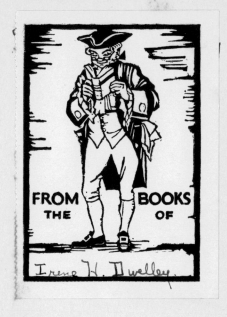

FROM BOOKS
THE OF

Irene H. Dwelley.

MAKERS OF EUROPE

LONDON : HUMPHREY MILFORD

OXFORD UNIVERSITY PRESS

MAKERS OF EUROPE

BEING THE JAMES HENRY MORGAN LECTURES
IN DICKINSON COLLEGE FOR 1930

BY

ROBERT SEYMOUR CONWAY

Litt.D., Hon. Litt.D., Hon. D.Litt., Dott. on.Univ., Fellow of the British Academy
Hon. Fellow of Gonville and Caius College, Cambridge
recently Hulme Professor of Latin in the University of Manchester
Commendatore della Corona del Regno d'Italia

CAMBRIDGE
HARVARD UNIVERSITY PRESS
1931

PRINTED AT THE HARVARD UNIVERSITY PRESS

CAMBRIDGE, MASS., U. S. A.

PREFACE

The general design of this short course of lectures is explained at the outset of the first; my duty here is to render thanks to some friendly authorities who have allowed me, in parts of these lectures, to make use again of material which they have already published wholly or in part. In the lecture on Caesar, Messrs. Benn Bros. have kindly allowed me to embody a page or two from the chapter on Caesar in the booklet on *Great Writers of Rome* which I recently contributed to a series which they have published. I have to thank further my friend Dr. Henry Guppy for kindly allowing me, in the lectures on Cicero and Horace, to avail myself of matter which has already appeared in the *John Rylands' Library Bulletin*, though in both cases with considerable modifications. The lecture on Vergil appeared in a somewhat different form in the Proceedings of the Classical Association in 1928, and was published separately as a pamphlet by the University Press of Manchester, which has generously allowed me to make free use of it here. For the index I am indebted to the skilled and experienced hand of my wife, Mrs. Margaret Conway, M.A.; and the promptness with which the lectures were prepared for the press is due to the speed and care of my secretary, Miss Rhoda C. Kitts. And to the very able reader of the Harvard University Press I render again my hearty thanks.

I hope I may also be allowed to record my gratitude to Dr. Mervin Filler, President of Dickinson College, for the great kindness which he showed me in all the details bearing on the delivery of the lectures; and my pleasure that one of them could be honoured by the presence of the revered teacher and scholar whose name they bear.

R. S. C.

St. Albans, England
February, 1931

CONTENTS

MAKERS OF EUROPE

MAKERS OF EUROPE

I

CAESAR THE DESTROYER

THE purpose of this course of lectures is to study the personalities of some of the ancient Romans who have left their mark most deeply on Western civilisation as a whole. In due course we shall be reminded of the events in which they had their share; but my object is not to relate history, but only to make clear how its course was changed by certain great men, and especially by their more personal characteristics. To three of the four of whom I shall try to speak, our debt is wholly of good. Such weaknesses as we may discover in them have had, it would seem, no historical consequences, or, at least, none but negative. For example, although Cicero's attitude of indecision towards the political riddles of his day prevented him from seeing any approach to their solution during his lifetime, and made his life appear a failure to his own generation, the nobility of his political teaching had its due influence later on.

But of the character whom I must try to picture first, that of Julius Caesar, it is more difficult to speak, although perhaps no figure in history has been the subject of more confident judgements formed by men impressed with this or that side of his amazing powers. Yet, as we shall see, on more than one vital question of his character raised by what he did, the ancient witnesses are silent, and even Shakespeare's lifelike portrait has, in these respects, nothing to tell us. On these points, the modern student of history, if he tries to be honest, will hardly expect to reach any clear and completely satisfactory verdict. I can only promise to make no statement that is not based on my own direct study of the ancient authorities.

Let us begin by acknowledging frankly the greatness of the man we are studying. As his worst enemy said of him, in Shakespeare's famous lines, whether sincerely or not,

> "Why, man, he doth bestride the narrow world
> Like a Colossus, and we petty men
> Walk under his huge legs . . . "

But the questions remain, in what did this greatness consist, and how far did it help or hinder the progress of humanity? It is, perhaps, too daring to try to answer them in a single lecture; and you may think that no one should judge Caesar unless he reckons to be as great a man himself. But after all, we ordinary people, for good or ill, are bound to form judgements of persons much greater than ourselves; and if a student evades the task by tamely accepting the last or the loudest verdict, he may, indeed, do no one any particular harm, unless his indolence proceeds to the point of retailing ill-founded statements unexamined; but he will certainly do no good; and I have to ask your indulgence if I speak frankly in the light of definite evidence, which is not indeed new, but which has been rather strangely suppressed. After all, David takes a risk when he attacks Goliath, and if his stone goes wrong, that will be the end of his attack. But I hasten to explain that the Goliath I have in mind is not Caesar, whose greatness, as I have said, is past dispute, though it needs examination. I am concerned to attack the judgements of a great scholar whose services to his own and future generations are far beyond ordinary praise; and yet who, in the one part of his writings which has exercised more direct influence on our time than any other, has been guilty — I can hardly use any other word — of so large a number of grave and clearly demonstrable errors, that for my own part I could wish that particular book publicly burnt in the playground of every school and college.

You will, perhaps, realise that I am speaking of Theodor Mommsen's *History of Rome*; and I must begin these studies by making clear — for it is still necessary to do so — the untrustworthiness of that famous book. The man in the street has taken its truth for granted because of the reverence with which he finds that scholars speak of Mommsen's work as a whole. That reverence was richly earned by half a century of splendid labour which has practically doubled for us the quantity of surviving Roman literature, by adding to it the records contained in fifteen or more enormous volumes of the Corpus of Latin Inscriptions, and by hardly less epoch-making contributions to our knowledge of ancient Coinage and ancient Law, and of a number of most difficult ancient manuscripts. Before such an achievement we journeyman-scholars can only stand in amazement and gratitude. But this does not make it less our duty to examine the conclusions advocated by this master of research when he turns to a different field, the world of men, not of things, to literature and politics, not merely editing and dating records. It is now some fifty years since I first referred to Mommsen's History, and I have rarely used a book from which it was more difficult to extract a sane and simple statement of fact.

On nearly all the great problems of Roman history scholars are now agreed that Mommsen's verdict was completely wrong. It is really difficult to discuss, even with the patience of respect, his extraordinary view that the Etruscans entered Italy from across the Alps, a theory contradicted by the whole evidence of archaeology as well as of tradition; or his no less strange belief, still unhappily accepted by some, that the difference between the Patricians and Plebeians of Rome did not imply a difference of race; or his complete failure to explain the origin of the different Classes in the Servian Constitution, save by the gratuitous assumption of a proprietary tenure of land for which there never was the faintest evidence; (Professor Ridgeway has since shown [1] that the Servian census was based on a different kind of property, namely, cattle). These are examples of Mommsen's errors in the earlier epochs; but all really spring from the same curious determination to reject the ancient evidence wholesale, especially that of the greatest Roman writers like Cicero and Livy. And when we come to the central period of Roman history,

[1] *The Origin of Currency and Weight Standards*, Cambridge, 1892.

the period with which these lectures will deal, his misjudge-
ments and distortions, as we shall see in one or two cases, are
quite grotesque. There is hardly a single figure among the
great writers of Rome except Horace of whom Mommsen
does not somewhere write with contempt; Vergil is to him
only 'the poverty-stricken Mantuan' — which is itself a mis-
statement;[1] and if in these few lectures I could achieve
nothing else but to persuade you to distrust every one of
Mommsen's judgements until you have examined the evidence for yourselves, I conceive that I should have rendered
a service to the truth.

The source of this unhappy obliquity in Mommsen's vision
of the period with which we are now concerned is perfectly
obvious, and, in fact, he proclaims it; namely the unbounded
admiration which he felt for the power by which the Caesars
established a united government in the Roman Empire;
and students of modern history have realised that this was
bound up in Mommsen's mind with his admiration for the
similar empire being established while he wrote in Germany.
Of Julius Caesar himself Mommsen always speaks as the
founder[2] of the Empire, in spite of the fact that Caesar's
policy led to his own death, and that to a renewal of fierce
civil war. Thus Caesar's aim is described as the 'highest
which man is allowed to propose to himself, the political,
military, intellectual and moral regeneration of his . . . nation.'[3] 'Political, military, intellectual, moral'— this is
what boys would call "a tall order," especially the last cate-
gory, in the case of a man who purchased by enormous sums
of money the support of nearly all the politicians who es-
poused his cause,[4] and who continually chose for his agents
worthless and abandoned persons like Publius Clodius and
Piso, the father of his wife Calpurnia. 'Caesar was monarch,'
writes Mommsen, 'but he never played the king . . . he was
monarch, but he was never seized with the giddiness of the

---

[1] In *Cosmopolis* (London, 1896, p. 545) a journal now extinct.

[2] See further p. 11 *infra*.

[3] *Roman History* (trans. by Dickson), 1887, IV, 453; *Röm. Geschichte*, 8th Ed.,
1889, III, 464.

[4] See e. g. Plutarch, *Caesar*, c. 20 (init.), c. 21 (med.), c. 29 (med.).

tyrant.'[1] Yet later on [2] we are truly told that Caesar had his own statue erected beside those of the seven traditional kings of Rome as the eighth, and appeared publicly in the costume of the old kings of Alba (which included a golden throne and a triumphal wreath)! 'He is . . . perhaps,' writes Mommsen, 'the only one of those mighty men who has . . . not broken down in the task of recognising, when on the pinnacle of success, its natural limits.' [3] 'Caesar was the entire and perfect man. . . . It formed part . . . of his full humanity that he was in the highest degree influenced by the conditions of time and place. . . . The perfect man just because he more than any other . . . possessed the essential peculiarity of the Roman nation — practical aptitude as a citizen — in perfection.' [4] Mommsen would really seem to regard Caesar's assassination as evidence that Caesar had recognised the facts of his position! Yet it was precisely because he had not enough aptitude to gauge the temper of his own fellow-citizens that the world had to wait another thirteen bloodstained years for the more patient and less arrogant Augustus. 'Although a gentleman, a man of genius, and a monarch, Caesar had still a heart.' [5] Mommsen's conjunction 'although' ("obgleich . . . dennoch") throws a rather amusing light on what he was accustomed to expect of gentlemen, and monarchs, and men of genius. 'To his wives,' Mommsen continues, '. . . he devoted an honourable affection' ("eine ehrliche Zuneigung"). We know nothing to show that Caesar was not fond of his wife Cornelia whom he married as a boy of seventeen; but the other alliances were purely political, and one was ended by divorce at a few hours' notice, merely on the suspicion of misconduct, as Caesar himself stated. But what Mommsen meant by an 'honourable affection' may be judged by his further statements (half a page later) which are undoubt-

---

[1] *R. H.*, IV, 455; *R. G.*, III, 466.
[2] *R. H.*, IV, 472; *R. G.*, III, 484. See also p. 17 *infra*.
[3] *R. H.*, IV, 456; *R. G.*, III, 467 ('those mighty men' alludes to the Biblical phrase "die Gewaltigen des Herrn" which Mommsen had used just before on p. 466).
[4] *R. H.*, IV, 457; *R. G.*, III, 468.
[5] *R. H.*, IV, 451; *R. G.*, III, 462.

edly true. 'Even in later years Caesar had his love-adven-
tures and successes with women,' ("Erfolge bei Frauen"),
to which he adds, by way, I suppose, of apology: 'However [1]
much, even when monarch, he enjoyed the society of women,
he only amused himself with them ("so hat er doch nur mit
ihnen gespielt") and allowed them no manner of influence
over him; even his much-censured ("viel besprochenes") relation to Queen Cleopatra was only contrived to mask a
weak point in his political position.'! This 'contrivance,'
as Mommsen calls it, was prolonged for six months [2] (October, 48–March, 47 B.C.) with consequences nearly fatal to all
Caesar's plans, as Mommsen elsewhere points out [3] frankly
enough.

You see that it is hardly necessary to go beyond the limits
of the History itself to find refutation of its extravagance.
Thus though we read that 'Caesar was the sole creative genius produced by Rome,' we are also told [4] that 'the ideas
which lay at the foundation of Caesar's work were not strictly
new; but to him belongs their realisation.' Yet this realisation was strangely deferred till fifteen years after his death,
and so far as it did happen, came about in a different form.
'Caesar's work was . . . salutary, not because it was or could
be fraught with blessing in itself, but because . . . absolute
military monarchy was . . . logically necessary and the least
of evils.' [5] This necessity was not recognised by the conspirators, who prevailed at least so far as to cause Augustus
to devise a totally different constitution, in which all the old
Republican forms, in particular the state-religion and the
dignity of the Senate, on both of which Julius had trampled,
were carefully preserved.

'As the artist can paint everything save consummate
beauty, so the historian, when once in a thousand years he
falls in with the perfect, can only be silent regarding it.' [6] Yet

---

[1] R. H., IV, 452; R. G., III, 463.
[2] Vergil clearly has this in mind in Aen., IV, 193, nunc hiemem inter se luxu quam
longa fovere. See further p. 14 infra.
[3] R. H., IV, 431 and 438–439; R. G., III, 443 and 449–450.
[4] R. H., IV, 450, 465–466; R. G., III, 460, 476.
[5] R. H., IV, 467; R. G., III, 478.
[6] R. H., IV, 457; R. G., III, 468.

we may observe that what Mommsen describes as 'silence' on the part of the historian has been maintained for eight pages![1]

We have lingered too long on these examples of Mommsen's loose statements, though I felt bound at the outset to show how necessary it is to consider the facts for ourselves. In the title of this lecture I have tried to indicate what appears to be Caesar's real claim to our gratitude, his work as a destroyer.

The evils that needed to be destroyed in the Roman Empire as it then stood, in control of all the world, though their general character is familiar to most of us, make a total which it is scarcely possible to describe. For in that terrible century before Augustus, 133 to 31 B.C., the sufferings of the world, caused by what Horace might well call 'the delirium of rulers,'[2] were such as even our generation can hardly conceive. In that period of time Italy had seen twelve separate civil wars,[3] six of which had involved many of the provinces; a long series of political murders, beginning with that of the Gracchi, and ending with Caesar and Cicero; five deliberate, legalised massacres, from the drum-head court-martial,[4] which sentenced to death three thousand supposed followers of Gaius Gracchus, to the second Proscription dictated by Mark Antony.[5] After fifty years men still spoke with a shudder [6] of the butchery of seven thousand Samnite prisoners in the hearing of the assembled Senate, and Caesar had also seen the last act of the struggle with Spartacus and his army of escaped gladiators — six thousand prisoners nailed on crosses along the whole length [7] of the busiest road in Italy, from Rome to Capua. As we shall see, the long

---

[1] *R. H.*, IV, 450–458; *R. G.*, III, 461–469.

[2] Horace, *Epistles*, I, 2, 14.

[3] Bellum Sociale; Bellum Octauianum; the return of Sulla; the wars of Lepidus, Sertorius, Spartacus, Catiline, Julius Caesar, the Triumvirs; in 41 B.C., the year before the Fourth Eclogue, the Bellum Perusinum; and after that, before the Georgics were published, the naval war with Sextus Pompeius and the final conflict with Antony.

[4] Orosius, v. 12.

[5] The three others were those of Marius and Sulla, and the execution of the followers of Spartacus.

[6] Caesar, ap. Cic., *ad Att.*, IX. 7c. 1.

[7] About one hundred and fifty miles; Appian, Bell. Ciuil. I, 120 *ad fin.*

record of the oppression of the provinces is not less terrible. The cause of this chaos was the breakdown of the old town-government when set to manage an empire. We note (1) a complete decay of civil control over the military forces of the empire, so that every Roman commander at the head of an army was tempted to engage in free-booting on the largest scale, since at Rome they were responsible only to the Senate, which consisted of men looking forward to or back upon the same opportunities of enrichment, and to the Popular Assembly, which could always be bribed or intimidated; (2) the concentration of capital in the hands of the governing class of Rome so that, speaking broadly, the creditors from whom the provincials themselves were fain to borrow were hand in glove with the military Governors, who were supreme in the provinces; (3) the economic consequences of perpetual warfare, especially the enormous growth of slavery, and the constant danger of slave-insurrections.

In face of the fierce resolve of the governing class to maintain these abuses from which it amassed enormous wealth, ordinary measures and ordinary men were useless. Things were bound to grow worse before they could grow better, worse in the sense that the defenders of the worn-out system must be resisted and defeated. They were deaf to appeals of either reason or humanity. In the penetrating insight and iron resolve of Julius Caesar, there was found, at last, a power of destruction equal to the task, and there can be no doubt that those were the qualities which the tyrant Sulla recognised in Caesar when he was a young man of seventeen whose death he had commanded, because the youth flatly refused to abandon his marriage with Cornelia, the daughter of one of Sulla's enemies. The noble relatives of Caesar bestirred themselves to secure his pardon, and Sulla gave way to them, grimly remarking that they might have their way provided they realised that 'inside Caesar's skin are three such men as Marius.' And Marius, as we know, except for his great reforms in the army, which had enabled him to protect Italy from the Barbarians, had been merely a force of destruction. The fundamental change which at last established good government in the Empire, namely the fixing of ample and graduated stipends for all classes of officers in the different provinces, was the work not of Julius but of Augustus, prompted, it would seem,[1] by Maecenas.

One incident in Caesar's early life, when he was scarcely twenty-five, is characteristic. During one of his periods of absence in the East, where he had fled from the hostility of Sulla, he was captured by pirates, who were masters of the Aegean. Plutarch[2] continues the story thus:

They asked Caesar only twenty talents for his ransom. He laughed at their demand, as the consequence of their not knowing him, and promised them fifty talents. To raise the money he despatched his people to different cities, and in the meantime remained, with only one friend[3] and two attendants, among these Cilicians, who considered murder as a trifle. Caesar, however, held them in great contempt, and whenever he wanted to sleep, used to send and order them to keep silence. Thus he lived among them thirty-eight days, as if they had been his guards rather than his captors. Perfectly fearless and secure, he joined in their diversions, and took his exercises among them. He wrote poems and orations, and rehearsed them to these pirates; and those who expressed no admiration he called dunces and barbarians. Nay, he often threatened to crucify them. They were delighted with these freedoms, which they imputed to a frank and facetious vein. But as soon as the money was brought from Miletus, and he had recovered his liberty, he manned some vessels in the port of Miletus in order to attack these corsairs. He found them still lying at anchor by the island, took most of them, together with the money, and imprisoned them at Pergamus. After which, he applied to the then governor of Asia, to whom it belonged to punish them. But he having an eye to the money, which was a considerable sum (over £12,000), would only promise to consider the case of the prisoners at his leisure. So Caesar returned to Pergamus, and, on his own authority, crucified all the prisoners, as he had threatened to do.

Of course, it was a hard world, a world which practised slavery and infanticide as well as crucifixion; which took its pleasure in watching gladiators kill each other and in which, when a town was taken in war, male captives were commonly

---

[1] Dio, lii. 23 and lxxviii. 22; cf. Tac. *Agric.* 42.

[2] *Caesar,* c. 2. Here and there I have corrected Langhorne's rendering, following the text of Sintenis (Teubner, 2nd Ed., 1881).

[3] His doctor, according to Suetonius, *Iul.* c. 4.

slain, the women and children enslaved. Nevertheless, there was something peculiar in the ruthless temper of a man who could crucify men with whom he had lived, though in captivity, on familiar terms; and we trace it again, in the 'mercy' which he showed to the men of Uxellodunum [1] on their surrender in 51 B.C. He spared the lives of those who had taken part in the rebellion, but cut off their right hands. He put his own cook into fetters for sending to table the wrong kind of bread; and he scourged and beheaded one of his own trusted freedmen because of an intrigue with the wife of a Roman knight, 'though no one,' so adds the historian, 'had made any complaint.' Whether Caesar had any personal ground for his act, we do not know; his own record in such matters makes it ridiculous to attribute to him any moral indignation; it was probably merely due to his patrician disgust at a freedman's having aspired to the favours of a noble lady.

Entering political life, Caesar took his place at once as the leader of what was called the popular party, which had, in fact, no positive ends, only the resolve to destroy the power of the governing class. Caesar became their leader, first by various revolutionary proposals, some of which he carried through, though others he merely flourished as a kind of red flag to encourage his supporters; secondly by profuse expenditure, such as an exhibition of gladiators, during his Aedileship, in which he put no fewer than three hundred and twenty pairs of combatants into the arena, and he grumbled [2] publicly that he was not allowed to exhibit a much larger number; for a law of that time had fixed that maximum. One result was that he was soon after in debt for more than 1300 talents,[3] roughly about £315,000 sterling (over $1,500,000). Another source of his popularity was the charm of his personal bearing. Thus he succeeded by the time he was forty-one, in reaching the Consulship, in alliance with the two most powerful persons then living, Pompey, who had subdued and reduced to order the whole of the Mediterranean and the

---

[1] B. G., 8, 44.   [2] Plut., c. 5.

[3] Plut., c. 5 (*prope fin.*) from whom we also learn (c. 11) that he had to secure a guarantee of 830 talents (over $1,000,000) from Crassus before he could leave for Spain as Proctor in 61 B.C.

eastern provinces, and Crassus, the millionaire miser, who was everyone's creditor.

For the next ten years the whole Empire was administered to suit the convenience of these three conspirators, whose agreement was kept a secret until it was broken by the death of Crassus, in 55 B.C., and it was never fully understood until it was finally destroyed by the quarrel which Pompey, in the hands of feebler adherents who belonged to the old gang, forced upon Caesar five years later. The result of this agreement was simply that the control of all appointments, whether to magistracies in Rome, or governorships in the empire, was in the hands of these three men. The forms of election by the Popular Assembly, and nomination by the Senate were retained, but the will of the Three was always enforced, by threats and military interference if bribery failed. By this single arrangement Caesar had destroyed the election of magistrates by the people, and the whole authority of the Senate, and the legislative powers of both bodies had fallen into the hands of these same three men, who now controlled in practice both the capital resources and the military powers of the whole community. Yet the idea of such control was by no means new. Gaius Gracchus, Saturninus, Marius, Sulla, Lepidus, Sertorius, and even Pompey, had all desired, and even won, a supreme authority of this kind; but it needed the amazing intellectual power and iron resolve of Caesar to give the *coup de grace* to the old system.

The result to Caesar himself of this Triumvirate, as it came to be called, was that he secured the province of Gaul for five years, from the beginning of 58 B.C. to the end of 54 B.C. The tenure was afterwards extended for another five years, and we know that he paid enormous debts and established his fortune for the future by the fruits of his command. But he did more than this. He made subject to Rome the whole territory which we now call France and Belgium, instead of the southern portion only; and he made two excursions in 55 and 54 B.C. to Britain, then first seen by Roman troops. His *Gallic War* he wrote some time between 52 and 49 B.C., when the Civil War began. Later on he wrote three books on the *Civil War* — the war into which he was driven by the jealousy of Pompey, and which lasted for five years, in every one of which he fought a great battle with his rivals and always won. These Books cover only the years 49 and 48 B.C., and are clearly shaped by the desire to show that the war had been forced upon him against his will. After carrying through certain modifications in the system of the Empire, some of which became permanent, Caesar was assassinated on March 15th, 44 B.C. His murderers had private reasons for hating him; by his laws all of them had lost their chances of provincial commands or contracts which they were handling or expected to handle in the old oppressive fashion. Yet they would probably have been powerless to effect the murder but for the fierce unpopularity which Caesar had incurred in Rome by trampling on many of the venerable customs of public life, and on not less deeply rooted ideas of what was respectable conduct.

One circumstance, which Mommsen and other modern historians ignore, is attested by contemporary evidence — the fact that, although Caesar was married to Calpurnia, who belonged to a noble Roman family, he had living with him in Rome in 44 B.C. the beautiful Egyptian queen Cleopatra, whom he had put upon the throne of Egypt only to become her slave. After his death, she, and not Calpurnia, was in control of his house; so Cicero's letters [1] show. This Shakespeare did not know, but his picture of Caesar's humble friend in the crowd, trying to tell him of his danger, is undoubtedly true. Plenty of people in Rome knew of the great conspiracy, but no one who stood near enough to him to be heard cared enough to take the risk of warning him. So perished, in his fifty-sixth year, the destroyer of the Roman Republic.

We naturally turn to his own writings in the hope of finding some notion of the person behind his political and military achievements. A passage describing the taking of Avaricum is a fair specimen of the narrative of the Gallic Wars:

[1] *Att.* xiv. 8. 1; xiv. 20. 2; xv. 15. 2.

A little before the third watch of the night the Roman soldiers noticed that their stockade was on fire because the enemy had attacked it through a mine; and at the same time sorties were made from two of the gates of the town. . . . Some of the defenders were throwing torches and dry brushwood on to the stockade, and pouring on pitch and other inflammable matter, so that it was difficult to judge at what point the mischief could be stopped, or where help should first be sent. Still, since by Caesar's rule there were always two legions on the watch outside the camp, and there were a large number of men engaged, shift by shift, on the rampart, no time was lost in meeting the sallies. . . . They cut through the rampart to prevent the spread of the fire; and the whole force was roused from the camp to put it out.

The fight lasted all night all along the line, for the townsmen felt that the deliverance of the whole of Gaul hung on the issue. An incident occurred under the eyes of the present writer [1] which appears to him worthy of record, and not to be passed over. One of the Gauls stood in front of the gate of the town throwing lumps of fat and pitch which were handed to him, straight on to the blazing tower in the stockade. Hit by a shot from one of our machines, he fell mortally wounded. The next man stepped forward over his body and continued his work till he fell in the same way, and was succeeded by another and yet another; and the place was never left vacant until at last we succeeded in putting out the fire, and the battle ended in the enemy's complete repulse.

Caesar then relates how the men in the town planned to desert it, leaving the women and children behind. But, on learning this, the women raised such an outcry that the Romans caught the alarm, and the Gauls desisted from their attempt, knowing that the Roman cavalry would beset the roads.

Next day there was a great storm of rain, and Caesar, having repaired the rampart, thought that the bad weather gave him an excellent opportunity. Accordingly he ordered his own men to go about their work with apparent carelessness, and then he went round the sheds, exhorting the legionaries to crown their long labours by victory at last, and promising special rewards to those who

---

[1] This English phrase may represent the equally stilted *nos* of the Latin, which Caesar, like other writers, affects when he speaks of himself as an author; for some account of this see my *New Studies of a Great Inheritance*, 2nd Ed., London, 1931, p. 4 ff. and the full discussion there cited (*Cambridge Philolog. Soc. Trans.*, Vol. V.)

should first surmount the enemy's wall. Then he gave the signal for battle, and they rushed out, all round the town, and speedily clambered up the wall.

We learn then how the enemy, seized with panic, threw away their arms and tried to escape through one of the gates; and the story ends thus:

Many of them were cut down by our soldiers while the gate was blocked with the crush. Others, who had made their way out, were cut down by our cavalry. None of the Roman soldiers stopped to secure plunder; and so resentful were they at the recollection of the disaster they had recently suffered and the toil they had had in the siege, that they spared none, neither aged men nor women nor young children. Of the whole population, which was about 40,000, scarcely 800 escaped to join Vercingetorix.

That is to say, 39,200 men, women, and children were put to the sword in one night! And Caesar writes as though he had no more responsibility for it than for a storm of wind or rain. From this measure, if you can, the total of human agony represented by Plutarch's summary statement:

In ten years war [1] he took 800 cities by assault, conquered 300 tribes, fought pitched battles at different times with 3 millions of men of whom 1 million were slain and 1 million taken captive and enslaved as prisoners.

From the *Civil War* take the brief chapter describing Pompey's murder as he was landing in Egypt after he had fled from the stricken field of Pharsalia:

The friends of the young king who were in charge of affairs . . . either in fear (as they afterwards alleged) lest Pompey should take possession of Alexandria and the kingdom, or in mere contempt for his unfortunate position, turning from friendship to enmity as men are wont to do towards their fellows overtaken by calamity, made answer openly with generous promises to Pompey's envoys, and bade him come to the king. But in secret they made a plot, and instructed Achillas, the king's prefect, who was a man of unusual daring, together with a Roman military tribune called Septimius, to murder Pompey. This man greeted him cordially; and Pompey, since he knew something of Septimius, who had been a centurion

[1] Plut., c. 15 *ad fin.*

under him in his war with the Pirates, was induced to embark on a small ship with only a few attendants; and there he was slain. Lucius Lentulus was also imprisoned by the king and subsequently put to death.

The facts are presented with no single indication that Caesar's own feelings were concerned in what he wrote; and this is, of course, deliberate. But it must be confessed that page after page of such guarded reticence makes rather dull fare, especially for a schoolboy who cannot penetrate below the polished surface. The story proceeds with a kind of even, impersonal flow, like water from a tap, and as if it came from some source outside the world of human events.

In truth this frigid, almost metallic, quality is Caesar's own mark. It is certainly true that he was capable of passion, capable, indeed, of being blinded by it. His love for Cleopatra all but brought him to destruction at Alexandria in 47 B.C.; and, as we have seen, her presence in Rome, and his yielding to her love for Oriental splendour in contempt of Roman sentiment, did prove fatal. He had set up a statue of himself at Rome inscribed 'To the unconquerable god'!

That he was fond of collecting other people's witty sayings and capable of witty sayings himself we know.[1] But he was a solemn creature, and of real humour he seems to have been destitute. What should we think of a modern general who telegraphed home the three words: *Veni, Vidi, Vici* ('I have arrived, I have seen, I have conquered')? Yet this was Caesar's report of the battle of Zela in 47 B.C., which he caused to be blazoned on a tablet and carried high in his triumph. This lack of humour is what makes his *Commentaries*, despite the praises they have enjoyed, such a dead expanse. The general clearness and historical value of the story are beyond dispute. It never rises; it never sinks; it is never angry or pitiful, and it never smiles. The result is, whether we read Caesar's own words or the reflection of him in other writers like Cicero, we feel ourselves in the presence of one of those

[1] Perhaps the best of his recorded sayings was when, in landing on the coast of Africa, he stumbled and fell — which his troops took as a bad omen. But Caesar grasped the earth and cried, "I hold you, Africa!" which made it a good one.

men who are born to be a riddle — enormously strong and capable, and gifted with a remarkable insight into his fellows; without sympathy with individuals, but enormously admired by those with whom he had to do at a distance — for example, by common soldiers or by his slaves — but never understood by his own relatives or friends, and detested as heartless by his enemies. Such men have often many reasons for what they do and say, and it is always difficult to know what feeling, noble or selfish, has governed them most. Caesar's personality remains in his writings the same enigma as it presented to his friends in life.

This uncertainty may seem disappointing, and, in truth, it is. But however we interpret his character, we must at least not forget three signal facts: First, that Caesar did practise a policy of amnesty on a large scale to his opponents in the Civil War, a policy which was at last adopted by Augustus when he had been converted from the savage cruelty which followed his first successes. Secondly, that everywhere he showed almost magical daring. The whole story of his wars makes it doubtful whether there was ever a commander who could so continually turn a defeat into success by dint of sheer determination, unquenchable courage, and brilliant enterprise, as Caesar could. Thirdly, and chiefly, that he had one quality whose attractiveness cannot be denied, though it was obscured by the brutality of the men whom he bought for his tools and associates, like Gabinius, Clodius, Piso, Dolabella, and Mark Antony, and by his own surrender at the end to a senile weakness for regal display. That quality has been best described by the saying that Caesar was a great gentleman. That is certainly true. There are records of many pointed and decisive utterances, such as his command to young Metellus, to stand away from the doors of the public treasury in 49 B.C., lest worse should befall him. But even that coercive act showed complete courtesy in form of speech; and the charm of his manner, and its effects on both citizens and barbarians is again and again recorded. Examples of this may be found in the two or three surviving letters which he wrote to Cicero in the first year of the Civil War, as well as in

Cicero's own description of the visit which Caesar paid to him on his victorious return, 'my unwelcome but not altogether regrettable guest.'

A case in which courtesy was blended with statesman-like wisdom was after the great victory at Pharsalia. The defeated Pompey left behind him all his personal belongings, including a mass of papers full of the names of his supporters, both avowed and secret, and all his plans for the future. These papers [1] Caesar promptly burnt unread.

Two minor, but pleasing, examples are given us by Plutarch. [2] One evening, in the provincial town of Milan, he and his suite were entertained at supper by a friend whose cook had poured stale oil [3] over the vegetables, instead of fresh. Caesar ate freely of the dish, but his companions plainly expressed their disgust, for which Caesar afterwards rebuked them, saying that 'to find fault with any failure of hospitality is to make such a failure yourself.' On another occasion, on the march with his lieutenant Oppius, who was ill, and several others, he was forced to take refuge for the night in a poor man's cottage where there was only one room. Caesar insisted that Oppius should have the room, while he and the rest of them slept under a shed outside.

It was this kind of conduct, combined with his splendid courage, that made him the darling of his soldiers; and it may at least incline us to believe, in spite of the ruthless severity which he often showed, in spite of his crucifying the pirates and of the horrors of Avaricum and Uxellodunum, that there did lie behind his policy of amnesty to Roman citizens, not merely the prudent calculations of a statesman, but at least some breath of humane feeling. It is at least to his credit that he [4] certainly wished men to believe it.

---

[1] Suet., *ad loc.*   [2] Ch. 17 *ad fin.*

[3] Suet. c. 53 *conditum* (i. e. *uetus*) *oleum*, which Plut., *loc. cit.*, renders by μύρου, taking the Latin word as the participle of *condīre*!

[4] On this see now Prof. Cornelia Coulter in *Class. Journal XXVI* (1931), p. 513 where the evidence of his coins, letters, and books is admirably discussed.

II

THE ORIGINALITY OF CICERO [1]

THE subject of this lecture was suggested to me by some remarks of my brilliant friend Professor E. K. Rand. In his book on the *Founders of the Middle Ages,* that is, on the great Latin writers of the fourth, fifth, and sixth Christian centuries, from St. Jerome to Boethius (and indeed to Charlemagne), Professor Rand again and again points out the influence which Cicero's philosophic writings had upon the Fathers of the Church, whose knowledge of Greek idealism, especially Plato's, came to them not directly but through Cicero. One point of Professor Rand's seemed to me to deserve further study than his immediate purpose allowed, namely, that all Cicero's teaching, though, as Cicero himself gratefully avows, it is based on what he had learnt from Plato and Aristotle as well as from later Greek thinkers like his own teacher Panaetius, was enlarged by his study of Roman history and his own political experience. Professor Rand rightly endorses the remark of Lactantius [2] that Cicero 'contributed a great deal of his own' (*nova ipse afferens plurima*).

For fear anyone should think that I propose to embrace the whole scope of Greek philosophy in this lecture, let me add at once that I can only deal with the political side of Cicero's teaching, and even that only in outline. In this field I hope to make it clear that Cicero's work was original, and in fact marked an epoch; and that its creative influence has continued down to our own times and is still important in the modern world; though that influence has spread through so many derivative channels that most modern writers have ceased to think of it as Cicero's at all. And since it has happened to me to be studying this subject in an interval between

[1] This lecture was first delivered at the John Rylands Library on March 12, 1930. I am indebted to my friend Professor J. L. Stocks for some valuable criticisms at the proof stage on several details which I have been glad to amend.

[2] Rand, p. 52. Lact. I. 2, iii.

two visits to the United States, it has a particular interest for me in this, that Cicero's teaching comprises several principles of government on which Englishmen and Americans are in complete agreement; and our agreement with one another, in theory and in practice, is, as far as I can judge, far closer than our agreement in such matters with any other nation in the world.

"Original" is, of course, a dangerous word. It ought to be used of discoveries which no one has made before; but then what is a discovery? If what the discoverer finds is something concrete and tangible, like the continent of America, which is then first brought within the range of human knowledge, we feel no difficulty. But after all, this is not the most important kind of discovery. Those discoveries which have brought about the greatest and most lasting changes in human life, from Copernicus to Rutherford and Marconi in science, from Zoroaster or Buddha to Wesley in religion, from Solon to Mazzini or Woodrow Wilson in politics, all have consisted in this, that their authors have seen new properties or capacities in things already familiar, or new and important relations between such things. The real question is as to the range and importance of the observation. I remember, from my early years at Manchester, a claim made by a clever young woman who has since become rich and well known from her contributions to a particular class of quasi-scientific literature. In those times she was a research-student in one of our departments, and she remarked one day at lunch that she counted a day lost on which she had not made a discovery; on which a highly distinguished physicist, who was sitting next to her, observed — to the delight of the table in general — "I suppose if you make a discovery on Monday and then find out on Tuesday that it is wrong, that will count as two?"

With this sobering recollection, I still venture to maintain that in the deepest sense of the word Cicero did discover important principles, because he took the brilliant inductions of Plato, which were based on the concentrated experience of the Greek States, and corrected them in the light of the growth of Rome and the Roman Empire. As we all know, Cicero was the leader of the Roman Bar, handling cases of public consequence, an administrator in one of the provinces, and soon the vindicator of that and other provinces against the intolerable oppression of their Roman governors; then himself chief magistrate of the Empire in a year of unique danger with which he had to grapple single-handed; later on himself a governor of one of the provinces on the border-line between East and West. So that even apart from the vicissitudes of his own career, he had been actually concerned in many capacities with the great adventure of governing the world.

It has often been the fashion to apologise for Cicero's treatment of Greek philosophy as being merely that of a translator, or at best, a compiler. This is because Cicero was essentially an eclectic; he took what suited his purpose wherever he found it; and he frankly disavows any pretence of erecting a single consistent philosophical system. His ambition is to write something which will be useful and help to guide men in practical affairs by connecting these affairs with first principles.

In his treatise *On The Republic* which, in spite of its fragmentary condition, is a most interesting book, he does not neglect the theoretical aspect of politics; only he is not concerned to elaborate any ultimate metaphysical or anthropological basis for his ideals. He takes over that basis from the Greeks — Plato, Aristotle, and the Stoics — as a matter of general agreement,[1] namely, the origin of society in the tribe and of the tribe in the family and the instinct [2] for social union, and then examines the principles of sound government, illustrating them from history, especially Roman history, down to the last quarter of the second century B.C.

Now what are these principles? If they are to be called discoveries it must be, as we have seen, because they are far-reaching. We shall find that they are at least so important that the freedom of our modern world depends upon them;

---

[1] *Rep.* i. 38, *illa elementa*, 'the abc of the subject.'
[2] *Rep.* iii. 35.

so that "The Modernity of Cicero" would have been an alternative title for this lecture.

John Stuart Mill's essay on Representative Government may, I suppose, be taken as embodying at least some of the main principles on which nearly all political parties in the free countries are agreed; and it is interesting to compare his canons of good government with Cicero's. Mill writes always with lucidity and humour, but he is wont to state his doctrine as the mere product of his own mind. He rarely refers to any of his predecessors except in the most general terms.

It is inevitable, I am afraid, that the points now to be considered will seem so familiar that you may think it hardly worth while to consider their history. One of the consequences of saying a thing well, as Pindar says, is that it "goes on with a voice sounding for ever"; and well brought-up young people who have imbibed some of these truths with their earliest lessons are startled when they come across them as they were formulated thousands of years ago. I remember a great saying of Horace which it is safe to say has comforted and strengthened hundreds of men [1] in terrible moments; yet it was quoted to me recently by a bright young student with the impatient exclamation, "How can people write such stuff!" Well, in Cicero's case, we should be fortunate indeed if we could regard his principles as finally established. Mill at least thought them worth contending for, and in the light of recent history it is hard to think that any free country can afford to forget them.

Let me put a few of these cardinal points in the form of questions.

1. What is a nation?

"A portion of mankind," answers Mill, "united among themselves by common sympathies which . . . make them co-operate with each other . . . and desire to be under the same government." [2]

---

[1] As young Quentin Battye fell mortally wounded on the ridge at Delhi, he murmured, in his last utterance to an old school friend, *Dulce et decorum est pro patria mori.*

[2] *Considerations on Representative Government*, People's Edition, 1867, p. 12 and c. xvi. init.

This is almost verbally identical, though Mill does not mention it, with Cicero's definition,[1] 'A state is not any kind of assemblage of men, but a union of a multitude of men, allied by consenting to the same law and by community of interests'; and more briefly, 'A state is a union of men to share the same law.'

2. What is the end of government?

"The well-being of the governed," says Mill, "is the sole end."[2]

This is again almost literally from Cicero. 'The ruler must look to the good of his subjects as a whole, not to his own advantage nor to that of any particular party.'[3] And he takes over Plato's illustration: 'The helmsman's object is a prosperous voyage, that of a doctor, health, that of a commander, victory; so the end of ruling a state is the happiness of its citizens.'[4]

3. What is the most important part of this happiness?

"To promote the virtue and intelligence of the people," says Mill.[5]

To the definition we have just quoted Cicero adds that 'the happiness of the community means that its position is secure, its resources adequate, its reputation honourable, its virtue high' — a fuller and rather finer definition than Mill's.

4. What is the chief way by which this is to be tested?

"The one indispensable merit of a government," says Mill,[6] "is that its operation on the people is favourable, or at least not unfavourable, to the next step which it is necessary for them to take in order to raise themselves to a higher level."

This is rather vague; Mill assumes that progress of some sort is essential to the life of a community and that the progress will be to "a higher level"; but he does not state in what the higher level consists, though presumably he meant to imply at least some progress in the sphere of morals.

[1] *Rep.* i. 39 and 49.   [2] *Repr. Gov.*, p. 12.
[3] *De Off.* i. 85 [and Arist. *Pol.* iii. 7. — J. L. S.].
[4] *Rep.* v. 58; of course modelled on Plato, *Republic*, i. 341 c. ff.
[5] *Repr. Gov.*, p. 12.
[6] *Repr. Gov.*, p. 15.

In Cicero's teaching the ethical ends of government are repeatedly indicated. For example, at the outset [1] he defines the impulse which leads men into public life as being 'the necessity,' that is the instinctive craving 'for virtue which Nature has implanted in men.' Thus the end of society is not ready made; it is something that has to be won by effort and development. And beside this we may set a noble passage [2] preserved for us at length by Lactantius which traces the ultimate source of government to 'the Law of Nature, the true Law, which is right reason in harmony with Nature, common to and binding upon all communities of mankind, past, present, and future, and which was devised and instituted by the Creator Himself.' This was a favourite doctrine of the Stoics, and Cicero, like other Roman lawyers, cordially embraced it. Thus he insists again and again [3] that there can be no government worthy of the name without perfect justice; and this does not come merely by Nature, i. e. not by birth, but is the natural goal of social order.

Thus the idea of perpetual change, which Mill seems to esteem for its own sake, is conceived in Cicero in a very different way, as we shall see soon.[4] Here note only that the final end of that growth is definitely stated by Cicero from a broader point of view than by Mill. It is true, I think, to say that Mill's standpoint throughout the book, like Hegel's,[5] is simply national. Mill regards himself as discussing the best kind of government for one particular nation. But Cicero at the outset [6] defines the greatest ambition of the politician as being 'to increase the resources of the human race' — not, observe, of his own state — 'and to make the life of men safer and richer' — not, you observe, only the life of his fellow-citizens, — *hominum*, not *civium* merely. That is a noteworthy difference, not merely from Mill, who might conceivably have accepted such a correction, but also from the point of view of the Greek philosophers from whom Mill as well as Cicero drew so freely.

[1] *Rep.* i. 1.   [2] *Rep.* iii. 33.
[3] *Rep.* ii. 70.   [4] P. 35 f. *infra.*
[5] P. 33 *infra.*   [6] *Rep.* i. 3.

We come nearer to our own everyday politics with the next two points:

5. What is the ideally best form of government?

"That," replies Mill,[1] "in which the supreme . . . power in the last resort is vested in the entire community, every citizen having a voice in the exercise of that ultimate sovereignty and being at least occasionally called upon to take an actual part in the government by personal discharge of some public function."

This is not far removed from Cicero's statement:[2] 'There ought to be in every community, first, some conspicuous and kinglike centre, next, some share alloted to the authority of leading men, and thirdly, some questions reserved for the judgement and decision of the whole mass of the people.' And these 'reserved' questions are matters of high importance.[3] 'Freedom has no certain home in any community except where the authority of the people is supreme. Nothing is dearer to men than freedom, and it cannot be called freedom unless it is evenly distributed.' Cicero dwells especially on the dangers of plutocracy, a danger which, though no doubt present to Mill's mind, is nowhere, so far as I have noticed, stated with more vigour and prominence than it is by Cicero, who declares [4] roundly that 'there is no more misshapen form of constitution than that in which the richest men are accounted the best.' Could any Labour member of Parliament express his democratic principles more strongly than this declaration written in 43 B.C.? Unless I mistake, nothing like it is to be found in Aristotle, whose attitude is very different, as we shall see; and though Plato's ruling class are superior in wisdom rather than in wealth, there is no doubt that they were to be comfortably endowed and under no necessity of earning their living.

6. How are the people to exert their influence?

[1] *Repr. Gov.*, p. 21.
[2] *Repr. Gov.*, p. 69 [Cicero's statement seems to me nearer to Aristotle than to Mill: it represents surely the general idea behind Aristotle's 'polity,' i. e. constitutional government. — J. L. S.].
[3] *Rep.* i. 47.
[4] *Rep.* i. 47 and 51. [Compare Mill's c. v. *ad fin.* — J. L. S.]

The answer which runs throughout Mill's book is, of course, that they elect representatives to the governing body. And Mill himself [1] points out that the Roman Senate escaped the characteristic disease of a bureaucracy, namely to be smothered in routine, through its popular element, that is to say, because its membership was determined by popular election to certain offices.

On this point Cicero repeatedly insists.[2] 'The way to place the welfare of the state in the best hands is that a free people shall choose the best men to govern them.' And again 'The people themselves, however wild and loosely organised they may be, nevertheless do possess a great power of telling one man from another, estimating them by many different qualities; and this power of choice is an important factor in their political life.' Elsewhere [3] he insists that 'unless the people as a whole have a share in such a choice they cannot be said to be free.'

7. What is the best security for continuous progress?

"The antagonism of influences," says Mill,[4] "is the only real security for national progress." In other words, the criticism of His Majesty's Opposition — in which, I believe, Mill took a joyful part in his day — is quite as important to the community as the initiative of His Majesty's Government, and it is a part of what Mill calls "mixed" or "balanced government" [5] in which decision is ultimately taken as the result of free discussion between representatives of different interests.

It is curious that Mill adds to this the note that "in the opinion of the Ancients a balanced constitution is impossible." But this very word balance (*compensatio*) is that used by Cicero [6] as being the indispensable condition of a stable constitution. There must be an even balance of privilege and duty, so that the power of magistrates, the authority of the body of leading citizens, and the freedom of the community at large shall all be properly shared. And similarly he indi-

[1] *Repr. Gov.*, p. 46.
[2] *Rep.* i. 51 and 53.
[3] *Rep.* i. 47.
[4] *Repr. Gov.*, p. 17.
[5] *Repr. Gov.*, p. 35.
[6] *Rep.* ii. 57.

cates, as we have seen,[1] that the best form of government will be duly 'combined and seasoned' from different elements; and Plato before him had realised [2] something of the same point. And we may say that the watchword of Cicero's whole political life, *ordinum concordia*, the harmony of the different orders, meant precisely this, the union of different interests by the process of discussion and conciliation, exactly the "give and take" which is the homely principle of British political life.

This point brings us face to face with the real basis of Cicero's convictions. Most of the seven principles of government which we have just examined — i. e. all but the fifth and sixth which insist on the people's share in power and on their exercising it by choosing their governors — are put by Cicero in a shape which was first given them by one or more of the Greek thinkers. But to say this does not answer a quite different question, namely, why did Cicero believe them? Why does he defend them with such enthusiasm? In a word, what is the source, not of his formulae, but of his intense conviction of their truth?

We may put the question in another way. Why does Cicero select these particular doctrines from the mass of political theory that he found in the books that he read, such as Plato's *Republic* and *Laws* and Aristotle's *Politics*? Why has it happened that Cicero's leading doctrines have entered into the life of the modern world and are still part of it? Many of the Greek doctrines that Cicero did not adopt but left wholly on one side are either still only on the fringe of practical thought or else have been unanimously rejected by practical men as having no place in the real human world. Why, for example, do we find nothing in Cicero of the regulations which both Aristotle [3] and Plato [4] solemnly debate as to the site of the community and its distance from the sea? Or of the number of its population, which Plato in his *Laws* [5] fixed as 5040, a number which he regarded as having beauti-

---

[1] See 5 above (p. 26).   [2] *Laws*, iii. 693. D. 2.
[3] *Pol.* iv. (vii.), cc. 6 and 11 (1327a ff.).
[4] *Laws*, iv. 704.   [5] *Ibid.*, v. 737 C.

ful mathematical capacities, and which Aristotle seriously
criticises as being too large? [1] We find in Cicero nothing of
the aristocratic limitation imposed by them both on the
franchise; for both Aristotle and Plato regarded it as vitally
important to restrict the power of voting, in other words, to
confine real citizenship, to a small, leisured and highly edu-
cated class. There is not much harm, says Plato,[2] in a carpenter's trying to do the work of a cobbler if he likes, but
'great harm may come from a cobbler's leaving his last and
trying to be a legislator.' And in the same spirit Aristotle
provides that all the physical work necessary for maintaining
the community is to be done partly by an inferior class, 'the
hangers-on' (περίοικοι), as he calls them, who are to furnish
among other elements in the population the farmers, the
sailors, and all the craftsmen, and partly by slaves, who, of
course, do not count.[3]

Nor, again, is there in Cicero anything of the topsy-turvy
regulations for marriage and for the restriction of population
which are given, though in different forms, both by Plato [4]
and Aristotle,[5] but which the general sense of every subse-
quent generation has rejected, as being not merely fantastic,
but, in Aristotle at least, altogether inhuman. And they are
strangely out of harmony with the general ideals which these
philosophers set before them. We may be allowed to observe
in passing that if even such thinkers as Plato and Aristotle
came to hopeless grief over the problems of sex, perhaps we
may learn a little patience in our own perplexities!

[1] *Pol.* ii. c. 6, 1265*a*.   [2] *Republic*, v. 458–461.

[3] *Pol.* iv. (vii.), c. 6 (1327*b*). In this both Plato and Aristotle had fallen far away
from the ideals of Pericles, who had boldly declared, in his great funeral speech of
431 B.C., that the Athenians 'claimed to be competent judges of politics without
neglecting their private business.' Plato and Aristotle held that Pericles' doctrine
had worked very badly at Athens, whose fall they attributed to its constitution.
This is a large question, into which I cannot here enter. They held that 'the life of
mechanics and tradesmen is ignoble and inimical to virtue,' and that 'husbandmen
have not the leisure necessary to the development of virtue.' (This was put more
briefly by Tennyson's *Northern Farmer* — "Take my word for it, Sammy, the poor
in a loomp is bad.") This Aristotle assumed as self-evident (*Pol.* vii. 8, 1328*b ad fin.*,
cf. Plato, *Laws*, xi. 919); but all the course and especially all the great crises of sub-
sequent history have shown that these Greek philosophers were wrong. There is not
a word of such doctrine in Cicero.

[4] *Republic*, v. 458 ff.

[5] *Pol.* ii. c. 6, 1265*b* and iv. (vii.), c. 16 (1335*b*).

Enough has been said to illustrate the kind of weakness in the great Greek thinkers which Cicero has completely escaped. In his own picture of the state he certainly achieved the kind of success which he hoped to do [1] in his conception of the after-life, a conception which had an immense influence on Vergil, on the Fathers of the Christian Church, on Dante, and indeed on all Christian thought. At the outset of that part of the *Republic* which we generally know as *Scipio's Dream*, we are told that what he has to say is put, not as was Plato's theory,[2] in the shape of an elaborate myth (told by a man who came to life again after lying nine days on his funeral pyre), but as a dream dreamt by a real person, the greatest statesman of his day, 'on purpose to suggest that the reader has not before him fantastic inventions, mere fables fit for derision, but the sober conjectures of thinking men.' Some day I should like to return to this beautiful vision; but here I must keep to the more mundane side of Cicero's work; noting only in passing how closely the religious and the political aspects of it are linked in Cicero's mind.

To come back then to our two questions. Why did Cicero believe so fervently in just these political doctrines and why did he choose these and leave aside so much else in his Greek mentors?

The answer to both is the same. It is that Cicero had learned the value of these principles by his own efforts to put them into practice, by the discipline of actual experience. As we leave the pages of Plato's *Republic*, beautiful and perennially stimulating as they are, still more as we turn from the cold reasoning of Aristotle, despite the value of his shrewd comments on Greek history, to Cicero's political writings, we feel that we have passed from the atmosphere of the study to the free air of actual life, passed from rainbows or cobwebs to reality. This could be illustrated at almost any length; a few concrete examples must content us now.

But first I beg your attention to one simple point. It repre-

[1] *Rep.* vi. 3.   [2] *Republic*, x. *ad fin.*

sents a movement in the world's history which took place after Plato's time, but which had begun under the eyes of Aristotle, in the achievements of his great pupil Alexander — though it seems to have made no impression on the mind of the philosopher. It had put a new face on the world before Cicero began to write, and it helps to account for the vastly enlarged horizon of political thought in which he moved.

It is of course the unique interest of Greek history to have provided the world with an object lesson in almost every kind of political development in the career of the City States. That institution was the birthplace of human freedom; and by a historical process which I have tried on other [1] occasions to trace, every free government the world has known has been ultimately descended from this Greek source. But the City State, though it did not disappear, had lost its pre-eminence in the three centuries between Plato and Cicero. No longer the single city but great conglomerations of cities, loosely called Empires, occupied the stage of the world. The difference between the old and the new can be represented by the history of a single word, the Greek word πόλις, 'city,' 'state,' 'community.' This one word, as many scholars have pointed out,[2] dominated the thought of Plato and Aristotle.

---

[1] See my *Great Inheritance* (1920), c. X.

[2] For instance, Susemihl and Hicks' Introduction to their edition of Aristotle's *Politics* (London, 1894), p. 46. So A. E. Taylor, in *Aristotle* (People's Books Series, undated but not later than 1920), p. 82 ff., writes: "The independent city state does not [i. e. in Aristotle's view] grow as civilisation advances into any higher form of organisation, as the family and village grew into it. It is the end, the last word of social progress. It is amazing to us that this piece of cheap conservatism should have been uttered at the very time when the system of independent city states had visibly broken down, and a former pupil of Aristotle himself was founding a gigantic empire to take their place as the vehicle of civilisation." And Mr. Alfred Benn, in his brilliant account of the *Greek Philosophers* (2nd Ed. [1914], p. 254), though his admiration for other sides of Aristotle's work is profound, states frankly the limitations of his political outlook, contrasting it with the fruitfulness of Plato's leading ideas, in spite of the fanciful shape in which these are embodied: "Not one practical principle of any value, not one remark to show that he understood what direction history was taking, or that he had mastered the elements of social reform as set forth in Plato's works: — the progressive specialisation of political functions; the necessity of a spiritual power; the admission of women to public employments; . . . the radical reform of religion; . . . the use of public opinion as an instrument of moralisation — these are the ideas which still agitate the minds of men and they are all those of the *Republic*, the *Statesman* and the *Laws* [of Plato]." On this Professor J. L. Stocks sends me the following note: "I entirely disagree with Professor Taylor's phrase 'cheap conservatism.' The city remained for a Greek under Alexander and under

Their highest and largest political dreams were all circumscribed by the walls of 'the city.' This one Greek word comprised the whole subject of their reflections; ἡ πόλις was the state, the body of citizens, the government, the country; there was nothing larger to care for or to reason about. But to Cicero the most natural translation of the word in Latin, the word *urbs*, means just what we today call a city [1] and no more. But beside it Cicero had to reckon with the term *civitas*, and the difference implied that the citizens of a state need not all live inside the boundaries of one town. He had further the word *respublica* to signify the economic and political aspects of a government; above all, the great Roman word *populus* which the instinct of the free communities of Europe has seized upon as containing the broadest and deepest connotations of any political unit. Greek has no such [2] word.

We are now prepared to observe, though briefly, one or two points which are especially characteristic and fruitful in Cicero's thought. You will hardly find them in Mill's teaching, certainly not in any prominence; and taken together they are still fresh enough to be of importance. The first, which we have already noted in passing,[3] was implied in the historical change just traced. Cicero's platform is not national but world-wide. *Roma* means to him not merely a city, nor even the capital of Italy, but the centre of an Empire; and the duties of government which he sets out to depict regard not the inhabitants of Rome or even of a single country, but the duties of the Roman people to all their allies, that is,

Rome the centre of loyalty, the lawgiver, etc. If you or Professor Taylor now put the question to Aristotle, he would have asked you what element the conquests of Alexander had added to the life of the citizen of Athens or Ephesus. Unless you could suggest some such element, he would have insisted that society completed itself with the πόλις. Of course I quite agree that the organisation of the Roman Empire opened up all sorts of new ideas.'' When philosophers differ so warmly, far be it from a mere scholar to intervene! But even Professor Stocks seems to admit that Cicero could have given a substantial answer to any such question as that imagined on the lips of Aristotle by his loyal defender.

[1] Cicero's definition (*Rep.* i. 41) is 'a collection of houses, marked out with temples and open public spaces.' This is interesting, and retains something of the social and religious sentiment which Plato and Aristotle found in the Greek word; and it may be cordially commended to our town-planning authorities.

[2] δῆμος is only a part, and generally a bad part, of the πόλις.

[3] P. 25 *supra*.

to all the peoples of the οἰκουμένη, the then known world. In one [1] passage he contrasts the ordinary ambitions of Roman governors (*fines imperi propagare; quam plurimis imperare*) with the higher conceptions inspired by a sense of justice, 'to show mercy to all, to care for the good of the human race, to render every man his own, to lay no hand on what is sacred or public or belongs to another.' "For the Greek all foreign nations were barbarians; for the Roman they were possible allies, potential subjects or citizens." [2] Cicero's conception of justice and order, of courts of law, of finance, of military discipline, of negotiation, in a word of all the departments of state, is shaped by his experience of the Roman Empire. Note two sides of his political theory which are closely connected with this oecumenic outlook.

First, his view of war. So far as I know Cicero was the first political thinker to lay down a doctrine which the world has not yet, or only since our last war, been willing to accept, a doctrine which you will not find in Plato or Aristotle or Hegel; for Hegel [3] assumes, as Plato appears [4] to do, that war is a necessary part of human existence; and from that Hegel deduced that the state was the supreme arbiter of morals, in short, that the state could do no wrong and that the citizen could appeal to no authority behind or beyond it. 'No war can be undertaken,' Cicero writes, [5] 'by the best kind of state

[1] *Rep.* iii. 25.

[2] Lord D'Abernon, speaking at the Hellenic Society's Jubilee, June 24, 1929.

[3] See Ernest Barker, *Political Thought from Spencer to To-day* (London, 1916), p. 29: "Hegel permits the State, as the highest expression of social morality, to escape from any moral restrictions. The state of war, in his view, shows the omnipotence of the State in its individuality." [Professor Barker is referring to such passages in Hegel's *Philosophy of Right* as *Werke*, viii. (Gans, Berlin, 1833), 258, 272, 324–334; Dyde's translation, pp. 240, 276, 332–334]. Kant, however, had been far nearer to Cicero's standpoint: "Kant, it appears, had little idea of the corporate life of a national State. The free will of the individual is the core of his thought. The State he conceives as in its nature a contractual body; and far from exalting the control of the State over the individual, he emphasises the necessary subordination of the State to the ideal of a permanent peace of Europe, and advocates a federal league of nations, each subject to the adjudication of the general collective will." (Barker, *ibid.*, pp. 26–27, referring especially to such passages as *Werke* [Rosenkranz], ix. p. 160, and to his famous book *Zum Ewigen Frieden*, translated by N. C. Smith, 1903.)

[4] *Republic*, ii, 373*d* ff., especially 375*b*, where the class of guardians is first named, and where their whole functions and training are based on the expectation of war.

[5] *Rep.* iii. 34 and 35.

except to maintain its good faith or its safety.' 'There can be no just war except for a punitive or defensive purpose.' These are principles of which we may be thankful to have heard a good deal more in the last ten years than humanity ever did before; but there they are, laid down by Cicero twelve years before the first Roman emperor rose to power.

"But how about the Roman Empire?" someone will say. "How could Cicero hold such a view and yet defend the possession by Rome, even in his day, of its unique power over the rest of the world?"

In precisely the same way as English statesmen have been continually bound to defend the existence of the British Empire, namely, by appealing to the historical principle which, speaking broadly, is true of both. The process by which they came into being was just that familiar to us in *Uncle Tom's Cabin* where, when she was asked about her origin, Topsy could only answer, "'Specs I growed." 'The mastery,' said Cicero, 'which our people hold of all the world has come in the course of defending its allies.'[1] I take it that that sentence would cover the greater part of the extensions of the British Empire in India and elsewhere, and not less of the expansion of the United States in past and in recent times. The central power, in order to protect its subjects and allies from the incursions of the wild men on their borders, finds itself continually obliged to bring those wild men themselves within the links of the same alliance.

This leads us to the second point of special importance in Cicero. It is one on which I have dwelt elsewhere,[2] and it is of great interest as showing the meaning which the best thinkers of Rome impressed on the conception of empire. According to Cicero the Roman Empire should have been called rather a protectorate (*patrocinium orbis terræ*),[3] for he realised fully how large a share in the life of that Empire was taken by the self-government which prevailed in all the allied

[1] *Rep.* iii. 35.
[2] In a lecture entitled "Ancient Empires and the Modern World," first given at Melbourne, Australia, in September, 1928, and at several places in the United States in 1929; now published as one of the Martin Classical Lectures of the University of Oberlin for that year (Vol. I).
[3] *De Off.* ii. 27.

states; and this example was taken deeply to heart by the real founders of the British Empire, especially by Lord Durham in his great proposals on which was based the constitution of Canada, the first of the Dominions to receive self-government.

And on Cicero's lips this phrase was not a mere word. It represented the greatest achievement of his life — the creation of a certain body of responsible opinion in Rome in favour of the just, temperate, and humane government of all the provinces. After Cicero's prosecution of Verres, and the great speeches in which he supported the grant of special powers in the provinces first to Pompey and then to Caesar, on the ground of the interest of the provincials themselves, this opinion, though continually trampled on, had come to have a force with which even the most reckless governor had to reckon before as well as after his own tenure of office; and quite certainly this opinion was a large element in determining the standard to which the government of the Empire was to be adjusted for four centuries to come. Augustus, no doubt, it was who first achieved the *pax Romana*; but it was Cicero who first conceived it and made it a reality in men's minds.

There is, further, in Cicero's whole treatment a note familiar in Plato and the great Athenian statesmen before him, but hardly or rarely audible in the cool survey of Aristotle. It is essentially Roman, represented in Latin by the word *patria*. To Cicero the relation of the citizen to the state was the relation of a child to his family. The citizen, he tells [1] us, must be 'trained' to think of his country as of his parents, and be prepared, indeed eager, to 'repay to his country the cost of his nurture.' This is, of course, the old and beautiful doctrine embodied in the Greek word τροφεῖα of which Plato makes full use. Cicero uses the word *amor* in his very definition of political life — 'such a craving for virtue and such a love for defending the common welfare.' And that was to be the end of education, to create this passion for the well-being of his country in the mind of every child. Where Aris-

---

[1] *Rep.* i. 8 and 33.

totle and even Plato regarded government, broadly speaking, as imposed on the subjects, Cicero has realised the secret of free government — that it is based on the personal confidence of the governed in their governors. He counted it a crime [1] that Caesar should carry in one of his triumphs the image of the city of Marseilles which had been for many centuries the faithful ally of the Roman people, but had sided with Pompey in the Civil War. Caesar's proceeding, said Cicero, and with perfect truth, was an example of the futility of government by fear; and he counts it an important feature of the virtue of justice that its possessor is sure to win men's confidence,[2] quoting name after name of great Romans who had held their power because they had won men's trust.

Here we are on the foundations, as Lord Morley of Blackburn would say. This brings us to the essence of Cicero's conception of the state, that like the family it was an organic growth. To Cicero the state was not what it seemed to Plato and Aristotle, just a city which had not very long ago attained its ideal of self-government and was always in danger of losing it again; it was a community whose progress towards new stages of organisation had been continuous for six or seven centuries, and whose task of civilising other nations had become more and more definite during the last of these seven. He speaks [3] of the historian as watching the Roman Republic 'being born and growing and reaching maturity, and now in the settled strength of manhood.' All this growth Cicero believed, as we have seen,[4] to have been inspired by the same creative spirit that shaped the beauties and wonders of the physical world. And if I mistake not, this organic element and the essential, formative, creative place in society of the principle of mutual regard, of the links between the members of the human family, is a cardinal point in the political thought of our own time.[5] It occupies a central place

---

[1] *De Off.* ii. 28.   [2] *De Off.* ii, 33.
[3] *Rep.* ii. 3.   [4] P. 25.
[5] See e. g. Professor Ernest Barker's interesting survey of *Political Thought from Spencer to To-day*, on T. H. Green, p. 34 ff.; on Hegel and Bradley, p. 62; on Bagehot, p. 151 ff.; on Graham Wallas, p. 151 ff.; on Maitland, p. 175. For Professor Barker's own conclusions see p. 246.

in Burke's thought, as Mr. A. J. Carlyle [1] reminds us; and the same is certainly true of T. H. Green and later writers. It has rarely been more finely stated than by Cicero: 'by nature we are disposed to love men and that is the foundation of law' (*natura propensi sumus ad diligendos homines, quod fundamentum iuris est*).[2]

"Well," you say, "of course Cicero profited by the experience of the Roman Empire. All you tell us comes to this, that just as Plato and Aristotle reflected experience gathered from Greek democracies when they had fallen on evil days, just as Hobbes reflected the value attached in the seventeenth century to the powerful rule of a monarch, just as Hegel,[3] followed in our own day by other German writers, consecrated the Prussian belief in power as something which justified itself, so Cicero's theory represents the ideals of Roman government." In one sense that is perfectly true. It is Cicero's glory to have seized on the best ideals of government which had grown up in the centuries of Roman history and which had been developed by Roman commanders and statesmen; and to Cicero more than to anyone else, with his student Livy, we owe their preservation in a permanent and articulate form.

But if the criticism means that these principles were actually in force in Rome and its Empire in Cicero's day, or indeed that anyone but Cicero in that age would have chosen to assert them, then nothing could be further from the truth.

Many lectures could be filled with stories of what the Roman Empire actually was in the last centuries of the Republic, under a corrupt Senate and its unscrupulous and mostly cruel representatives. So far from expressing the opinion of his day, Cicero's teaching was in fierce defiance of it. He was in opposition all his life. Even in his consulship he had to fight anarchy almost alone; for those who applauded his courage at the moment refused afterwards to take the least share of the responsibility. Consider only a few examples of the evil methods which had become ingrained in the Senatorial government.

---

[1] *Mediaeval Political Theory in the West* (London, 1903), Vol. I. c. 1 *ad. fin.*
[2] *De Leg.* i. 43.   [3] See p. 33.

Some of the towns of Asia Minor had purchased at a great price from Sulla, when he was in need of money during the war with Mithradates, immunity from the recognised forms of tribute paid by provincial communities. The Senate, on the proposal of one of its most responsible leaders — a man called Philippus who in private seems to have been quite respectable — cancelled the immunities and yet refused to restore the money, a proceeding which Cicero rightly stigmatises [1] as immoral.

At about the same epoch — somewhere in the seventies B.C. — a man called Dolabella was governor of the province of Cilicia, and in pursuance of an agreement with Verres, whose character even then was notorious, an agreement [2] for which Dolabella must have received a large bribe, appointed this Verres to conduct an official mission to the king of Bithynia. To embark on this enterprise Verres, as a Roman envoy, demanded a ship from the town of Miletus. They provided him with one of the brand-new ships-of-war which they had built for use against the pirates, in accordance with their treaty with Rome. In this fine vessel Verres sailed to his destination in the Hellespont; on his arrival he dismissed the crew of Milesians to make their journey home over several hundred miles on foot, and sold the ship to certain persons who promptly sold it again to the pirates. Such was the officer sent to represent the majesty of Rome at the court of Bithynia. And his proceedings went completely unpunished. Dolabella had golden reasons for making no remarks — 'a great ox had trodden on his tongue,' as Æschylus would say.

Or take the case of Calpurnius Piso, Caesar's father-in-law and Caesar's tool in banishing Cicero, one of the 'fine pair of Consuls' in the year 58 B.C., the first product of the secret coalition which we call the First Triumvirate. In 56 B.C. Piso reaped the reward of his subservience in the governorship of Macedonia, which then included some authority over the whole of Greece. We may note, by the way, that Piso ultimately attained to the office of Censor, the highest guardian of public morals, in 50 B.C., and that he lived and

[1] *De Off.* iii. 87.   [2] Cicero, *In Verr.* II. i. 86 ff.

flourished as late as 44 B.C., when he asserted successfully the right of making public his great son-in-law's will in spite of the protests of Brutus and Cassius. It is clear, therefore, that the Republican system protected this gentleman completely. We may believe, if we like, that his conduct in his province was a little less abominable than it is painted in the lurid descriptions of Cicero.[1] But however we judge him in details, the methods by which he amassed a fortune are instructive and beyond doubt. When he left Rome for his province he drew from the treasury a sum for his necessary outfit. This was eighteen million sesterces, i. e., £144,000 or $700,000 at the lowest computation, enough to furnish, I imagine, at least two or three, or for all I know a dozen, Viceroys of India. But in fact Piso wasted none of it on uniforms or transport; he laid it by in prudent investments before he left Rome. At the end of his time, when he left the province, he contemplated applying to the Senate for a triumph, — although on second thoughts he decided that that would be imprudent, since he had never even sent in any report to the Senate of his supposed military achievements. Nevertheless, he had spread it about his province that he expected to celebrate a triumph; and on that ground exacted what was called *coronarium*, that is, a sum of money raised by the different towns to express their joy in the successes and distinction of a departing governor. How much he got from the province as a whole is not recorded; but from the Achaeans alone he secured the trifling item of 200 talents, $240,000 at least. This, however, caused a little difficulty in his accounts, after he had decided not to apply for a triumph. But a man of Piso's resource was quite equal to the emergency; he simply entered the sum under other headings (such as provision for his journey or the like).

But Piso, you may say, doesn't matter much to us — though he mattered a great deal to Cicero. Let me remind you of a more famous example,[2] the noble Brutus. The better part of the Senate had at one time passed a rule for-

---

[1] *De Prov. Cons.* §§ 4–14; *In Pisonem*, passim, especially §§ 83–91.

[2] Cic., *ad Att.* v. 21; vi. 1 and 2, with Tyrrell's Introduction to Vol. III. of his and Purser's *Cicero's Correspondence*, pp. xxix and 337.

bidding members of the Senate to lend money to provincial communities; but the town of Salamis in Cyprus wanted to borrow, and a man called Scaptius, agent for Brutus, arranged to lend them what they wanted on his patron's behalf. Since the loan was illegal and might be cancelled if it were detected, the noble creditor was, sadly, obliged to charge them rather a high rate of interest — forty-eight per cent. After five years, the town council found itself unable to pay this modest rate, so to jog their memories Scaptius secured, by the usual means, the loan of a troop of cavalry from the governor of the province. These gallant horsemen, carrying Roman standards, shut up the town council of Salamis in their own town hall until five of them had died of starvation. The rest no doubt decided to pay the interest. The military power of Rome was thus applied to enforce in the cruelest way a transaction forbidden by Roman law, and nothing more is said. Cicero was governor of the province in the next year and cut down the rate of interest to the ordinary legal maximum of twelve per cent, refusing to lend cavalry to Scaptius. But even Cicero was not strong enough to cancel the whole transaction or to expose so great a patriot as Brutus; that would have violated the *ordinum concordia*. Against such oppression, it is only fair to say, Julius Caesar also set his face — at all events in other people's provinces — and many of his murderers had some score against him on this ground.

Another and graver example,[1] from the conduct of Verres in the embassy to Bithynia, shows how completely the Senatorial government was in league with evil-doers. When Verres arrived at Lampsacus, where he was to stay for some days, he ascertained, by his usual means, that a wealthy citizen named Philodamus had a beautiful daughter. It was the custom for Roman envoys and their chief men to enjoy the hospitality of leading citizens of the towns where they stayed. So Verres proceeded to impose on Philodamus the task of entertaining the precious chief of his own precious staff, a man called Rubrius. Philodamus, though he was

[1] *In Verr.* II. i. 61 ff.

most unwilling, thought it his duty to Rome to provide ample hospitality; but he sent his son out of the house in advance so that he need not associate with the kind of men whom Verres took about with him. At the end of the banquet Rubrius suggested that Philodamus should bring in his daughter, to which the unhappy father replied that that would be contrary to all the rules of Greek society. Thereon some of Rubrius's companions whom Philodamus had generously allowed him to bring, began to clamour, and Rubrius posted soldiers at the door of the house to prevent anyone leaving it. Philodamus realised that violence was intended and a slave escaped by a back door to warn his son. A riot ensued. Rubrius and his crew were turned out and one of the lictors, that is one of the official military footmen attending on Verres, was killed. The mob proceeded to the house where Verres was staying, and would have set it on fire over his head, but for the efforts of several Roman merchants living in the town, who pointed out to the crowd that that would only make matters worse; it would involve the most serious consequences if an actual Roman legate suffered violence. So Verres escaped and betook himself again with a full purse to his patron Dolabella, governor as we have seen, of Cilicia. So full was the purse and so great the urgency that Dolabella deserted his province (although he was responsible for a war that was then proceeding), and visited the governor of the province of Asia, a nobleman called Nero, who, according to Cicero, was a man of high character but 'unfortunately timid.' Dolabella represented to Nero the outrage committed in the slaying of a Roman lictor at Lampsacus, and prevailed on Nero to arrest Philodamus and his son and try them himself; and he further secured that the panel of advisers with whose help Nero was to try the case should include both Dolabella and Verres himself. Seeing Verres on the bench no citizen of Lampsacus dared to testify to the facts. Both Philodamus and his son were condemned and beheaded.

Here was a shameful outrage defended, and two totally innocent men put to death, by the joint efforts of two governors of Roman provinces, who between them held sway over the whole of Asia Minor.

I am loth to extend this catalogue of crimes; but you will not realise how integral a part of the Republican system of empire they were without one more example [1] from the career of our friend Verres, which his performances under Dolabella had not hindered in the least. One of the incidents of his governorship of Sicily was the capture and destruction by the pirates of a Sicilian fleet sent to fight against them. I need not tell you all the miserable story of why Verres appointed a worthless man to command the fleet, and how he thinned the numbers of its crews by accepting fees from a large number of the sailors to release them from service, the result being that the admiral's ship took to flight and the rest were driven ashore, deserted by their crews, and then set on fire by the pirates. Look merely at the end. In order to divert from himself and his local admiral the disgrace of the capture, Verres arrested all the commanders of the ships, young men of high family, tried them in his own court, sentenced them to death and executed his sentence. Observe in particular his method of making money out of the tragedy. The unhappy parents of the young captains went to the prison begging to be at least allowed to see their sons, and from these unhappy persons, through his jailor, Verres exacted great sums of money on four separate counts; first, to be allowed to visit the prisoners; secondly, to be allowed to take in food and clothing for their needs; thirdly, for a promise from the jailor that he would behead them at one blow and not dispatch them by slow torture; and fourthly, that he would allow their bodies to be buried and not thrown to the dogs. This is not a bad dream. It was actually carried out by the Roman governor of Sicily (73–71 B.C.) and on his return all the power of Roman society and Roman official influence was exerted to prevent this inhuman monster from being condemned. And even when, thanks to Cicero, who made brilliant use of the fears of members of the Senate in a political crisis, Verres was condemned to exile, he kept his

[1] *In Verr.* II. v. 82–121.

wealth, save only what he had been obliged to spend in pay-
ing his counsel Hortensius and other powerful senators for
their help, and in his vain endeavours to pay the jury of
senators enough to get them to acquit him.

Such were the principles on which the Empire had come to
be governed in Cicero's time; and you must engage in long
study if you would realise the enormous courage and determination which were needed to secure the condemnation.
Verres was defended by the most distinguished member of the
Roman Bar, and for his acquittal the most elaborate intrigues
had been set on foot to secure bribable consuls, a bribable
prosecutor, a bribable judge, and a bribable jury. But
Cicero succeeded in defeating them all by his fearless resistance and by the unprecedented speed with which he
collected and presented the evidence, so that the trial was
concluded in the year before that for which Verres and his
friends had been preparing.

But Cicero stood alone. Under the secret conspiracy,
known as the Triumvirate of Caesar, Pompey, and Crassus,
formed in 60 B.C., every honest or even intelligent principle
of government seemed to have perished, forgotten and con-
temned in the fierce struggle between individuals for political
power and the enormous wealth which it brought. The chaos
had lasted for a century, and it was no small thing even to
maintain in theory the standard of just administration; it
was a greater thing to have vindicated such standards at
grave personal cost in two cases like those of Verres and
Catiline; but Cicero did more. More was demanded of him
by the cruel conditions of his day. It was not only that he
had thought and worked and lived for his great ideals; he
must die for them too.

It has been the custom of recent historians to overlook the
historical importance of the stand which Cicero took. These
modern writers have been blinded by the brilliant but Prus-
sian-headed eloquence of Mommsen, who failed to distin-
guish between two quite different things: on the one hand, the
necessity of a centralised government; and on the other hand,
the unscrupulous and generally brutal violence practised in

their own interests by the ambitious persons who cleared the way for the Empire by destroying the Republic. It is time that, like Octavian himself, we recognised the truth. In 43 B.C. Octavian gave way to Antony and consented to the murder of Cicero; but some thirty or forty years later when he found one of his grandsons reading Cicero, and when the boy instinctively tried to hide the book, thinking that the emperor would disapprove, the emperor took it and gave it back, saying: 'That was a great man, and he loved his country.'

But in 43, though Octavian knew that he owed to Cicero's support his first step to power, he let himself be driven to consent to Cicero's death.

Few of the violent ends that have come to great men have been more full of tragedy. Cicero's murder came at a moment and in a fashion which signified to him that every one of the great ideas for which he had lived was crushed and extinguished. He could not know that his denunciation of Antony's tyranny and his brave pleading for a just and humane administration of the Empire was destined fifteen years later to remake the world. The appearance of Antony's cut-throats in that narrow forest path down which his faithful slaves were carrying him in the vain hope of escape, meant to Cicero not merely the end of his own life; that he nobly faced, refusing to allow his slaves to suffer by defending him. It meant also to him the overwhelming defeat of everything for which he had lived.

Fate seemed to laugh aloud at all his principles. "Society founded on community of interest"? All the power of Roman society was now in the hands of a greedy ruffian. "Society to be guided by law"? Every law in the constitution was suspended by the authors of the Proscription. "Society to be directed to moral ends"? Two thousand citizens were being put to the sword that their property might be transferred to these three men of blood. "The end of government should be to make life safer and richer and to increase the resources of mankind"? Every single province and all the wealth of the world was being ravaged in the greed of the usurpers. "Freedom to be tested by the voice which every citizen should have in determining the course of government"? Every voice, even the most eloquent, was beaten into silence, the Empire broken up, the Senate overpowered, Rome enslaved, the whole world at the mercy of armies led by tyrants. Such was the horizon on which Cicero's eyes looked in his last moments, and such was the appalling misery which he died to relieve.

Make no mistake; nothing short of his heroic resistance and death would have sufficed. It would have been easy for him to throw in his lot with the conquerors, as he had been continually entreated to do for all the last ten years of his life. If he had done so, who can doubt that the character of the Empire would have been wholly different and infinitely less beneficent? Indeed it would be truer to say that the Empire itself could never have been securely founded, until some other voice, if Cicero's had failed, had been raised to assert the supremacy of justice and humanity, to assert it with equal power and at equal cost. To Antony's vile designs Cicero's death was a necessity. In a deeper sense it was an even greater necessity for the political salvation of the world.

III

HORACE'S FARM AND ITS POLITICAL FRUIT

PREFATORY NOTE

THIS lecture is based, by permission, on two lectures published in the *John Rylands' Library Bulletin*, Manchester, in 1928 and 1929, entitled respectively "The Country Haunts of Horace," and "Octavian and Augustus." When it was delivered at Dickinson College, the first part was illustrated by views of the remains of Horace's Sabine farm and the surrounding country, which my friend Mr. G. H. Hallam, of S. Antonio, Tivoli, kindly permitted me to show. I do not feel justified in trespassing so far on his kindness as to reproduce them here, since the most important of them are easily accessible in his own book called *Horace at Tibur and the Sabine Farm* (Harrow School Bookshop, 1927), which ought to be in the hands of every lover of Horace; and he has generously presented to the "Society for Roman Studies" a complete set of slides, illustrating both the Sabine farm, and what seems certainly to have been a house, or *pied à terre*, of Horace at Tivoli in his later life, a site now occupied by Mr. Hallam's own villa.

THE site of Horace's farm in the Sabine hills has recently been placed beyond all doubt. It is impossible to find a place which would fit in more exactly with all the details which Horace gives us; and the conclusions drawn from the literary evidence have now been borne out by the results of excavation on the spot. To his Sabine farm and the fountain of Bandusia and to Mt. Lucretilis Horace makes at least thirteen quite certain allusions and five or six others that are probably so to be interpreted, scattered over all the works he wrote after 33 or 32 B.C.

Horace mentions his possession of this Sabine retreat for the first time in the Sixth Satire of the Second Book, when he wrote to thank Maecenas for the gift. 'That was what I prayed for; a measure of land not very large, with a pretty garden and a spring of pure water hard by the house and a little bit of woodland too. But the gods have given me something richer and better. It is good. I pray for no more than to be allowed to keep it.' He describes his migration there as 'escaping out of Rome into the mountains and my own cita-del'; and in the later part of the Satire he describes his simple life, free from all the burdensome fashions of the city; 'nights and suppers fit for the gods' he calls them, in which, after a meal in which his slaves take part, he has some friend to talk with on quite serious subjects, interrupted occasionally by a neighbour who tells them a pretty fable of the country-side in the manner of Æsop. Twelve years or more later on he sets out to describe the same farm to another friend, Quinc-tius. 'If you found,' says he, 'a gap in the line of mountains, thro' which a valley with plenty of shade runs north and south, you would call it an excellent situation. Even the trees and bushes of the hill-side are kind enough to bear cornel-berries and plums; and both oak and holm-oak are there to shade me and feed my pigs with acorns; and the slope is so warm that you would think you were in the woods at Tarentum. There is a spring that deserves a name of its own, as cold and as pure as some long winding river of Thrace; with water excellent for a tired head or an uneasy stomach. It is a charming retreat, lovely, I shall call it, if you will take my judgement, and it keeps me well all through the burning days of September.' Notice the word 'lovely' (*amoenus*, the prettiest epithet in Latin) that Horace applies no less than five times to the scenery around the farm, here, as you see, with a little apology. No doubt the comparative treelessness of the higher parts of the mountains round about, and the many rocks which break the grass, and occasional stony screes which take the place of grass in some parts of the lower slopes, presented less attraction to a Roman eye than they do to ours — in these things Horace has what I must call a very English sort of taste; but in any case, to Monte Gen-naro, the ancient Lucretilis, no traveller of our own day, if indeed, of any day, could possibly deny the epithet. The colour and shape of its purple rocky peaks and grassy sides, and the towering majesty with which it rises, its broad sil-very slope glowing in the morning sunshine and spreading for miles down the valley, are all lovely.

Starting from this a Rhineland scholar, Herr Nikolaus Fritsch, in the year 1895, after a stay of two months in the valley, condescended on a particular patch of land as the only one that suited what Horace said — the most striking point being that it was the only place in the whole valley where vines could grow and are now growing. Since then the site has been excavated with interesting results, which have entirely sustained Fritsch's conclusions. The remains of the house and garden suggest plenty of comfort; and perhaps you will smile with Juvenal and say that Horace could very well write pleasant poetry in such a pleasant retreat. That may or may not be true; but it does not by any means exhaust the significance of the farm in Horace's history. For remember how his life as a man had begun; — called to join the army of Brutus and Cassius after the murder of Caesar in 44 B.C. when Brutus was passing through Athens where Horace was then a student, he had fought on the losing side at Philippi and returned to Italy, pardoned indeed, but ruined — his father's estate having vanished in the confiscations. After that, some ten years of drudgery as what we should call a clerk in the lower Civil Service, drudgery relieved by his love of writing verses and latterly by his acquaintance with Vergil and Maecenas which these verses had brought him; and then the drudgery suddenly at an end for ever. But even that was not all. So long as Horace was in poverty every day's experience reminded him of the cause of his misfortunes — the Civil War not yet over, though it could now injure Horace himself no further. No wonder that in his early poetry Horace's reflections on public affairs are sombre and bitter. His generation seemed to him to be simply mad — all the more because he had for a time shared the madness. But now he was not merely pardoned but the injury done him by the confiscations had been redressed, no doubt with the consent of Octavian, who had himself been one of the authors of those confiscations; and it is not surprising that Horace conceived new hope for the future. These hopes were based on a great change which was in progress from 39 to 27 B.C., by which the unscrupulous and

ruthless Octavian was converted into the benign Augustus.
The difference in these two names marks a whole epoch in
history. How did the change come about?

If we are to judge the scope of the question, we must form
some picture of what kind of person Octavian was when at
the age of nineteen he succeeded to the name and a large part
of the prestige of the murdered Dictator — Julius Caesar.
There is no lack of evidence; we know that his entrance on
public life was made possible by the kindness and support of
the venerable republican statesman Cicero, who with real
foresight saw in his apparent docility and high-mindedness
a defence for the empire against the designs of ruffians like
Mark Antony. In the end Cicero's foresight was justified —
thanks to the strength in Rome of the spirit of which Cicero
in his lifetime was the greatest representative, but for the
moment it was to be rudely disappointed; and Cicero was to
be the first victim of Octavian's shattering bad faith. Cicero's
later *Philippics* give us a clear picture of the steps by which
Octavian became the commander of an army, put into the
field by the Senate, expressly to defend the empire against
Antony; and we all know how having used these forces to
defeat Antony at Mutina in 43 B.C., Octavian made friends
with him and agreed to the Proscription. The historian
Appian has preserved for us the text of the proclamation by
which the Proscription was announced; it was signed by
Lepidus and Antony and Octavian also. History gives us
many examples of tyrants and dictators who climbed to
power by a *coup d'état*, not shrinking from bloodshed; but it
is not so common for them to leave behind a public document
proclaiming their murders over their own signature. Yet
that is what Octavian has done. Let us consider some part
of this strange document which ended the first Act of the
drama of Octavian's public career.

We, Marcus Lepidus, Marcus Antonius, and Octavius Caesar,
having been elected to bring into harmony and order the affairs of
the Republic, make the following proclamation. . . . Seeing that
the wickedness of those who have plotted to destroy us, and by
whom Caesar was slain, cannot be overcome by any kindness, we

choose to anticipate our enemies rather than to suffer ourselves. Therefore let no man think us guilty of unjust or cruel excesses when he remembers the fate of Caesar and the wrongs that have been done to us. . . . Some of the murderers we have already punished; the rest with God's help you shall shortly see chastised. We have already succeeded in the greatest of our endeavours, and made subject to us Spain and Gaul, and the districts nearer home. One task yet remains: to make war upon the murderers of Caesar who are across the sea. And since we intend to conduct this war at a distance on your behalf, it does not seem to us to be safe either for us, or for you, to leave the rest of our enemies here behind us, since they would take advantage of our absence. Nor do we think that in the present emergency, we ought to be slow to act from any consideration for them, but rather we must put them one and all out of the way. We have no grudge against any large body of citizens, nor shall we make any choice of our private enemies nor shall we in the least single out those who are wealthy or politically eminent, though it must needs be that three men must have more enemies than one; we shall not slay as many as did the last Dictator, whom you called Sulla the Fortunate, although he too was called on to rule the city during a civil war. And though we might arrest those whom we know to be evil without warning, we prefer rather to proclaim their names for your sakes, so that, having them properly named and numbered, the soldiers may abstain from interfering with anyone else. Therefore, with the blessing of heaven, we give command that none shall give protection to any of those whose names are written below. Whosoever shall attempt to save them is included in the list. And whosoever shall bring the head of any one of them to us, if he be a free man, shall receive 2500 drachmae,[1] but if he be a slave he shall receive 1000 drachmae,[2] his freedom, and all the civic privileges of his master. The same reward shall be given to anyone who shall give information of their place of hiding. We shall not enter on our records the names of any who earn these rewards.

Then followed the 2000 names of the victims.

A share in this massacre, one would have thought, might have satisfied the cruelest mind; but Suetonius has collected from the same period other examples of Octavian's temper. A year later, after the battle of Philippi, he had all the distinguished prisoners brought before him and not merely had them put to death in his presence but insulted them first.

---

[1] Roughly $500 or £100.   [2] Roughly $200.

One man begged Octavian to allow him to be buried, to which Octavian replied 'that was a matter for the birds.' A father and son were brought before him, begging for mercy; but he made them cast lots as to which should be spared; then the father offered to die and was executed, and the son killed himself — all under Octavian's eyes. A year later still, at Perusia, when he had taken a multitude of captives and they besought him for mercy, he replied to each of them in the brief formula *moriendum est* — 'you must die.' Three hundred of them he selected from the senators and knights, and had them put to death as if they were beasts brought for sacrifice, at an altar built there to the honour, or dishonour, of the Dictator Julius.

It is pretty clear that from 44 to 41 B.C. the proceedings of Octavian were such as to make us ask whether we should think of him as one of those monsters to whom cruelty for its own sake is a pleasure. That is what we should have said if his record had ended there.

Now look at the other end of the story — Augustus contrasted with Octavian. Here also we have a signed statement of his own view of what he had accomplished for the world; and whatever opinion we may entertain of his motives, there is no doubt that these things were done. Of this autobiography, we possess a copy in Latin and one in Greek, each incomplete but serving to make good the gaps in the other. It was found at Ancyra in Asia Minor (the new Turkish capital Angora) and it has been much studied of recent years. Prof. W. M. Calder discovered a new copy in 1930. The inscription is headed by the statement that it is a copy of one cut on two brazen pillars set up at Rome, recording the deeds of Augustus by which he made the world subject to the Empire of the people of Rome, and the money which he spent upon the Roman state and people. Augustus then speaks in his own person and begins by a brief narrative of his punishment of the conspirators down to his defeat of Brutus and Cassius in October, 42, and continues thus:

I undertook the responsibility for conducting the Civil and Foreign Wars all over the world. I was victorious, but I spared all

Roman citizens who survived, and I chose rather to preserve than to exterminate all foreign nations who could be pardoned with safety. I sent home to their own towns, or established in colonies, considerably more than three hundred thousand soldiers who had served their time, and I gave to every one of them a grant of either land or money.

Later on he boasts of having three times closed the Gates of Janus because the empire was at peace, though in all the previous history of Rome they had only been closed twice. Among his benefactions he mentions with particular pride the sums he had paid [1] for the land that he gave to his veterans after the Civil Wars were over. (He might have added that he had joined in very different proceedings only thirteen years earlier, in 42 B.C.).

His description of his own change of name comes at the end.

After I had extinguished the Civil Wars and become supreme by universal consent, I handed over the government to the power of the Senate and the Roman people; and in return for this service the Senate gave me the title of Augustus ('Venerable') and ordered the doorposts of my house to be wreathed in branches of bay and a crown such as is given to those who have saved the lives of their fellow-citizens to be fixed over the lintel. Further a golden shield was set in the Julian courthouse with an inscription stating that it was given to me by the people and the Senate of Rome for valour, clemency, justice, and piety.

So the Imperial artist pictured himself; so he certainly appeared to the world from 27 B.C. onwards — a world which gasped with thankfulness that such a ruler had at last appeared to put its affairs in order. What produced the change?

In the fourth lecture of this course I shall try to trace the influence of Vergil. Let us consider now the different, though parallel influence exerted by Horace. Horace, as we know, was a friend and ally of Vergil's, a younger man, and not so deep a thinker, or so great a poet. Yet one who for all he was worth, and with persistent courage, pleaded for wisdom and humanity, a pleader especially persuasive because he was a

---

[1] See p. 73 *infra*.

man of the world as well as a patriot, with fine taste and a keen sense of humour, as well as a keen sense of what was right.

What kind of persuasion did he and Vergil exert? How did they succeed? I believe the answer to be closely connected with a fact of psychology of which history furnishes many examples, namely, the close kinship in the region of human motive between cruelty and fear. No man is so cruel as the man who is himself in terror.

After the murder of Julius Caesar it is easy to believe that his young heir felt more deeply than anything else the continual danger in which he lived and moved. Every street corner might disclose some assassin waiting to cut him down. To practise on a vast scale, as Augustus ultimately did, a policy of amnesty and forgiveness after a Civil War which has lasted for generations, requires in the first place courage, and in the second place courage, and in the third place courage. That is why it is so rare. It is very easy to entertain sentiments of humanity, in thought, or in word; it is a very different thing to dare to act upon them. Here precisely lies the essence of what Vergil and Horace did. By degrees they inspired Octavian with faith in the future of the Empire, faith in the value to the world of the task which had come into his hands to do, and courage to accept and continue it, instead of retiring into private ease, as Sulla had done, and as Pompey had tried to do. They infected him with their own confidence; they lashed the pilot to the wheel. Let me illustrate this from a few passages of Horace's *Odes* whose full significance has not been realised.

Horace's influence may be said to have been centered in three great refusals, as I have pointed out elsewhere.[1] Of two of these I have since found further illustration which I desire to submit to you now.

The first refusal was that like Mr. Rudyard Kipling, he

[1] In the lecture on "Horace as Poet Laureate," p. 52 of *New Studies of a Great Inheritance*, 2nd Ed., London, 1931. I have borrowed from that lecture, with some modifications, the passage describing the lifelong resistance which Horace offered to the ostentation of wealth. No account of the contribution which Horace made to the civilisation of Europe could be complete without it.

would not forget. Dr. Verrall [1] and others have pointed out the resolute loyalty which Horace maintained to the old Republican ideals and to old friends on the Republican side who had taken longer than Horace did to be reconciled to Augustus; the majority of the men to whom the Odes of Book II are addressed are of that number, like Pollio, Grosphus, Varus, and Dellius; and his guarded but striking tribute to Cato in the First Ode may be said to represent the spirit of the whole Book.

But neither would Horace, on the other hand, forget the danger from which Rome had at last escaped, and which more than once seemed likely to return. The most important example is an Ode about which even the latest editors are still in doubt, the Fourteenth Ode of Book I, in which Horace warns a storm-tossed ship not to venture out of harbour. This warning, Quintilian tells us, had a political meaning; but there has yet been no agreement among students of Horace as to what storm it was that the ship of state was bidden to avoid. Let me give you a rendering, modified from that of Conington.

> Oh ship, beware. New tides will bear thee swift
>   Back out of harbour; make the anchor fast.
>   Stript of thine oars, adrift,
>   — Seest thou not? — In thy mast
>
> The southern gale has left an ugly wound;
>   The sailyards groan, nor can thy keel sustain,
>   Till lash'd with cables round,
>   The too imperious main.
>
> The canvas hangs in ribbons, rent and torn;
>   No gods are left to pray to in fresh need.
>   A pine on Ida born
>   Of noble forest breed
>
> Thou vauntest name and lineage — mad and blind!
>   Fresh coats of paint no sailors' fear allay.
>   See lest the mocking wind
>   Make thee anew its prey.

[1] *Studies in Horace*, Cambridge, 1884, p. 100.

Sick with despair and longing, still I crave
Thy safety, though the blue Aegean smiles.
Beware smooth tides that lave
The rock-ringed Cyclad Isles.

A year or two ago, when I had occasion to study more
closely than I had hitherto the ancient authorities for the
history of the reign of Augustus, I stumbled on what I am
convinced is a real clue to the meaning of this Ode. For I
found what I ought, no doubt, to have found long before,
that Book LII of the history of Dio Cassius was taken up with
an account of a conversation between Octavian, his great
commander Agrippa, and his counsellor Maecenas, the patron
of Vergil and Horace. This took place in 29 B.C., and the
subject was the question what Octavian was to do. He had
just returned to Rome from the East for the first time after
the battle of Actium, and had celebrated his three days of
triumph over all his enemies. He thought quite seriously of
taking the advice given him by some of his friends, of whom
Agrippa was the chief, to resign all his powers, to become
merely a private citizen and to restore the Republican government. Agrippa's chief point, so far as Dio represents it,
was the invidious position of a monarch contrasted with the
great glory that would attach to the restoring of a free constitution.

Against this Maecenas replied that the Roman Empire
was too vast a system to go back to the old Republican
way of changing its rulers every year; and that it was not
necessary for the Emperor to expose himself to the envy
and ill will which the Dictator Caesar had provoked; and
went on to advocate the dual system which in fact Augustus practised, a monarchy limited by the forms of Republican government; the Emperor was, in a sense, to keep
himself always in the background. We know from other
authorities also that Augustus thought seriously of resign-
ing his power; but on the whole it seems certain that it
would have been a misfortune for the world if he had done
so. His retirement would only have meant a new outbreak
of civil war.

Now what side did Horace, the old Republican, take in this great question? We might have expected him to support Agrippa, or at least to be silent. But there seem to be strong reasons for believing that the danger against which Horace was warning the ship of state was the danger of Octavian's retirement. This explanation was, in fact, suggested long ago by the Dutch editor Torrentius, in 1608, and adopted by the German scholar Franke,[1] on the ground of the reesmblance between one passage in Dio's account of the debate and this Ode of Horace. But they offered no further evidence; and scholars generally seem to have treated the likeness as accidental. Dean Wickham recorded the suggestion without comment, and the best of all recent editors, Dr. James Gow, does not even mention it.

But in reading that book of Dio with Horace's *Odes* freshly in mind, I found a number of other points in which Dio's account of what Agrippa and Maecenas said tallies so closely with the political utterances of Horace as to make it difficult to believe that the two records are independent. Dio wrote two hundred years after Horace died, but no one has ever questioned his good faith or his careful study of the best authorities, like the Memoirs of Augustus. Modern historians seem to regard him as entirely trustworthy, except in the matter of omens and portents, where his view, though earnest and sincere, was that of his own age, far less critical than our own. If Dio thought that Horace was warning Octavian not to retire, we can hardly doubt that Dio was right. The parallels I have noted seem to show clearly that in all this book Dio was again and again thinking of different Odes of Horace. Besides the passage about the ship there are at least thirteen others in which he draws upon Horace.

The study of literary parallels is apt to be rather fatiguing, but the proof in such cases, if there is any, must be cumulative;[2] no one resemblance, nor even two or three resemblances, taken alone, afford strong enough basis for more than conjecture. But a string of them is a different thing.

----

[1] See p. 61 *infra*.

[2] The parallel passages side by side in Latin and Greek will be found appended to the lecture on *Octavian and Augustus* cited on p. 46.

We all remember Horace's boast,[1] that he has reared a monument more lasting than bronze; in Dio's account[2] Maecenas bids Octavian not to allow men to represent him in gold and silver images, but by his good deeds to carve undecaying and imperishable images in the hearts of men. (The conclusion reminds one also of Horace's praise of Lollius,[3] who is to be remembered not as the consul of one year, but as a good and faithful judge who continually set honour before profit).

In one of the last three Odes that he addressed to Augustus, Horace calls him *bonus* (*dux bone*), an almost familiar and quite surprising epithet addressed to an emperor. Maecenas uses the Greek equivalent χρηστός in a pointed exhortation[4] in which he tells the Emperor he must live up to his reputation of being a really 'good' honest citizen, totally unlike the bandits and revolutionaries who plagued the world before him and whom he has overcome.

Horace counts it a glory of the older Roman society that private fortunes were small though the commonwealth grew great; so Maecenas is represented as counting[5] it one of Octavian's claims to public veneration that he has been most thrifty in all his private expenditure, but most open-handed in his expenditure on public objects.

In praying for the Emperor's health[6] Horace hopes that he will celebrate great triumphs here on earth, and live long to be called father and chief citizen (*pater atque princeps*). Maecenas[7] encourages the Emperor by saying: 'Of course they will look to you and love you as father and as deliverer when they see you living a seemly and happy life, successful in your wars but a lover of peace.'

In another passage where the title 'father' recurs, Horace exclaims: 'Whoso will seek to have his name inscribed on statues as father of the cities, let him take courage to curb our lawlessness so long unchecked.' That is exactly the command[8] which Maecenas gives to the Emperor in Dio's version, to 'put a stop to the recklessness of the multitude.'

---

[1] 3.30.1. [2] 52.35.3. [3] 4.9.38.
[4] 52.18.4 and 35.5. [5] 52.29.3. [6] 1.2.28.
[7] 52.39.3. [8] 3.24.29.

In a famous passage, finely rendered by Conington, Horace exalts the man of real virtue whose dignity and glory are destined to be immortal, and contrasts these with the cheap honours obtained from the applause or the votes of the crowd.

> True Virtue never knows defeat:
> Her robes she keeps unsullied still,
> Nor takes, nor quits, her curule seat
> To please a people's veering will.
> True Virtue opens heaven to worth:
> She makes the way she does not find:
> The vulgar crowd, the humid earth,
> Her soaring pinion leaves behind.

How does Maecenas put it in Dio's prose? [1]

'See to it that those who take in hand some responsibility be chosen for their virtue, not by process of vote and canvassing for office. Virtue has raised many men to the rank of gods, but no man was ever made a god by a popular vote.'

Enough, I think, has been said to show that some of Horace's most cherished themes are represented in Maecenas' speech. But turn now to some coincidences in smaller matters which perhaps are even more convincing.

In celebrating the achievements of the Emperor's stepsons Horace [2] points out that brave men spring from brave sires, but that they need training too, to bring out their native qualities. Exactly the same combination appears in the speech of Agrippa in Dio's account: [3] 'What good can a man do who lacks either training or good birth?'

To this subject of education Horace recurs frequently. 'The minds of the young which in recent generations have been left to grow too soft must now be shaped by sterner pursuits. Our well-born youths are too untrained to keep their saddle, are afraid to engage in hunting, and far more skilled at games like trundling a hoop or gambling on the dice-board which our laws once forbade.' Notice the point that the aristocratic youth is proud of skill in something, but not of skill in the right things; and compare with that the

---

[1] 52.15.3. and 35.5. [2] 4.4.29. [3] 52.8.7.

exhortation of Maecenas which Dio thus represents: [1] 'You should give no one an excuse to take to idleness or soft living or excellence in any sham kind of skill.'

In another famous passage Horace puts his exhortation in a positive form.

> To suffer hardness with good cheer,
>   In sternest school of warfare bred,
> Our youth should learn; let steed and spear
>   Make him one day the Parthian's dread;
> Cold skies, keen perils, brace his life.

Or, more literally, 'he must spend his life in the open air and amidst dangers.' This is very like Maecenas' injunction [2] in Dio's prose: 'the young soldier must be reared so as to be always under arms, perpetually practising the duties of war even in wintry weather.' Still closer to Horace is the injunction that 'so soon as they grow to be youths they must turn to the use of horse and weapons, so that they may be trained to do their duty as men, from their youth upwards, both in theory and practice.' The exhortation to teach boys to ride had always sounded to me a little curious in Horace; a detail rather unimportant, so it might seem, as compared with the virtues of courage and simplicity which Horace is commending in the rest of the poem. But when we find exactly the same detail insisted on in this speech of Maecenas, and when we remember the interest that Augustus took in the new feature which he established in the Games at Rome and which he called the Trojan Sport, the performance of difficult equestrian feats by a squadron of boys of high birth, we see that this question of horsemanship meant a great deal. It is, surely, difficult to doubt that it was typical of the practical counsels which Maecenas actually gave to Augustus and which Horace here reflected.

These quotations are enough to show how similar is the colour in many passages of Dio's record of this conversation and in what we may call Horace's official Odes, which after all are not very many in number. It is difficult to reckon more than ten or a dozen at most.

[1] 52.26.4.   [2] 52.27.

But the strongest resemblance of all between the speech of Maecenas in Dio and Horace's teaching occurs precisely in the Ode we are studying. There are only twenty lines in the Ode, and only eleven lines in Dio's Greek; and in these eleven lines there appear to me to be five clear reflections of Horace's words, and four or five others, less close but probably real.

How unlikely this is to be the work of chance may be seen very clearly from the fact that although, as the ancient commentators tell us, Horace is imitating a Greek Ode of Alcaeus (of which they quote nine lines), there are only four resemblances between Horace and Alcaeus and only one which is really vivid, namely, the 'torn sails' of which both poets speak. The other three likenesses consist merely in the mention of 'mast,' 'winds,' and 'sailing' which must appear in any poem concerning a ship in difficulty.

Horace's picture is of a ship in harbour which is imprudently attempting to put to sea again in a storm. The image in Dio is rather different; there Maecenas definitely appeals to Octavian not to leave the helm. Without the captain the ship will come to grief.

The ship is borne on tossing waves; 'don't you see?' asks Horace; 'for you do see' says Maecenas. 'The mast has sore wounds from the wind' says Horace; 'the ship is rotten' says Dio. 'It cannot last any time longer' says Dio; 'it can hardly last' says Horace. 'The sea is overpowering' says Horace; 'the sea is gaining on the ship' says Dio. 'Your sails are no longer what they were' says Horace; 'the State has suffered now for many generations' says Dio. 'A ship of Pontic pinewood' says Horace, 'though the name does it no good'; 'a ship of great burthen' says Dio. 'It will be a sport of the winds' says Horace; 'it is rocking this way and that' says Dio. 'You must shun the waters between the shining Cyclads' says Horace — the Cyclads were famous for their reefs; — 'take care you do not let your ship be wrecked on a reef' says Dio.

Looking at leisure through these points one can hardly resist the conclusion that Dio is paraphrasing in his sober prose the picturesque details of Horace's poem. Franke [1] thought the likeness so patent as to need no comment at all.

Now if Horace ventured to publish such an utterance on *Independence* the very highest and most vital point of imperial policy, no less than the position in the state of the emperor himself, it is clear that his influence with the emperor was a thing to be reckoned with. And we are justified in attaching importance to his utterances in considering the forces which modified Octavian's conduct. Especially is this the case when we remember the personal independence which Horace stoutly maintained, from the early Epodes when he has nothing but condemnation for the ruling powers and shows not a little of his old Republican sympathy, through all his Odes, where he consistently honours men who fought against Caesar as well as those who fought on his side; down to the very end of his career when he refused the entreaties of Augustus that Horace should become his private secretary; and when in response to Augustus' request for a poetical letter addressed to himself, sent him only the Second Epistle of the Second Book, which is entirely occupied with technical literary questions and might have been addressed to any cultured Roman.

Now consider another of Horace's refusals, which is above all characteristic of his temper. He refused to be content with appearances, refused to accept the picture of external splendour which impressed the world around him. He pierces beneath the show to what is real. In a word, he is the enemy of vulgarity; for that is what vulgarity means, to take the shows of things for their essence; and in this lies the secret of the refining power of his poetry. *Persicos odi, puer, apparatus;* a poet and a gentleman must dislike and distrust the vulgarities of ostentatious wealth.

There is a striking example of this attitude in a poem whose meaning has been rather strangely unnoticed. It is a common experience, I think, that there is no occasion which unlooses so many springs of vulgarity as the opening of new buildings. Recall for a moment the kind of things that we hear (if we do not say): 'What a fine building, to be sure!

[1] *Fasti Horatiani*, Berlin, 1839, p. 152.

how good to think that we can afford it! how generous to have found the money! how clever to have been born now and not in the time of our unenlightened grandfathers! what a cultured community we may claim to be!' Or perhaps, if the buildings have some religious object, our comments take an even more solemn tinge: 'How good to erect such a structure for such an object! how worthy the building of its purpose! what a splendid conception it should afford of the object of our worship!' And the underlying thought that is not often put into words, but is nevertheless transparent, is something like this: 'When you come to think of it, really, how grateful and pleased the Higher Authorities must (in reason) be that we should have taken so much trouble for their sake!'

Now the greatest of all the buildings of Augustus, — that which commemorated one, indeed two, of his greatest victories, which crowned the most conspicuous hill in Rome, — was the Temple of Phoebus Apollo with its Library on the Palatine. It was first vowed in 36 B.C., dedicated in 28 B.C., and provided with a portico in 24. Let us see what the poet Propertius has to say about it:

You ask why I come to you so late? The golden Porch of Phoebus has been opened by great Caesar. All the porch was laid out with Carthaginian columns of marble to ample length, in the spaces between which was the crowd of the daughters of old Danaus. Here I saw a figure that surely seemed more beautiful than Phoebus himself, as he opened his lips in song, a singer of marble with a silent lyre. And around the altar stood Myron's drove, four artistic bulls. Then in the midst rose a temple of bright marble, dearer to Phoebus than his ancestral home Ortygia. Upon which was the Sun's chariot above the gable peak; likewise the doors, a famous piece of handicraft in Libyan ivory tusk, did mourn, one for the Gauls cast down from Parnassus' Peak, the other for Tantalus' daughter Niobe, and all her deaths. Anon there was the god of Pytho himself between his mother and his sister, in a long robe, making sound in song.[1]

---

[1] II, 31; I quote Prof. Phillimore's translation, modifying only his rendering of *femina turba* and omitting his second 'between.'

In these 16 lines there are at least four otiose epithets (*magno, tota, artifices, claro*), two prosaic relatives and four meaningless particles, including *atque* at the beginning of a line. Marble is mentioned three times, — really four times, since the

What does Horace say of the dedication of this temple to Phoebus? Consider Ode XXXI of his First Book in Conington's version:

> What blessing shall the bard entreat
>   Of new-shrined Phoebus as we pour
> The wine-cup? Not the mounds of wheat
>   On some Sardinian threshing floor;
> Not Indian gold [1] or ivory — no,
>   Nor flocks that o'er Calabria stray,
> Nor fields that Liris, still and slow,
>   Is eating, unperceived, away.
>
> .   .   .   .
>
> Oh grant me Phoebus, calm content,
>   Strength unimpaired, a mind entire,
> Old age without dishonour spent
>   Nor unbefriended by the lyre!

In other words: 'Grant me the modest competence I now have, but not increased; health of body and a mind unclouded; an old age free from avarice or regret, and always cheered by poetry.'

'Turn your thoughts away,' says Horace in effect, 'from such material display as you see before you; pray only and strive only for the real blessings which will not decay.'

Let me end with a point perhaps of smaller importance; yet it has a significance of its own. Among the resemblances between Horace and Dio, we saw a passage in which the Emperor was bidden, as Pericles bade the Athenians, to desire a memorial in the hearts of men, not in monuments of bronze. Set by that a statement in the autobiography of

---

uestis of the last line was also of marble. The last statement that Apollo 'makes sound in song,' contains a feeble and colourless use of *sonare* with a personal subject which represents unmistakably the writer's profound weariness. Would the song have been any more real even if the 'robe' had not been a 'long' one? Scholars have disagreed about the order of the couplets, and with reason. Nowhere in the poem are there any four lines which could be put at the end without seeming wholly trivial. The only trace of poetry is one fine couplet (ll. 13–14) in which the splendour of the carver's art has lifted the poet for a moment into a region of sincere feeling.

For details of the exact site of this temple and of the successive stages of its erection, I may refer to Prof. O. L. Richmond (*J. Rom. St.*, IV [1914], p. 200).

[1] Horace hated ivory and gilded ornament. (Cf. *Odes*, II, 18.)

Augustus from which we have already learned much. 'About eighty silver statues representing me' so the Emperor writes, 'some on foot, some on horseback, some in chariots with four horses which had been erected in Rome, I removed myself and melted down, and from the money hence derived I dedicated a gift of gold to Apollo in his temple, in my own name and in the name of those who had erected the statues to me.' Here you have an act after Horace's own heart;[1] an act which is rare in the annals of human autocrats.

Perhaps you will say that after all Horace does speak of reverence paid to Augustus at a divine level. And further that since Apollo was Augustus' chosen patron saint, to honour him was to honour Augustus under another name. There is truth in both these statements. Note, however, that Horace couples Augustus after his death not with Apollo, but only with other great benefactors, originally human, like Hercules and Romulus; and while he is alive, only with the humble and almost nameless spirits of the fireside, the Lares, to whom the countryman says grace, so to speak, at his evening meal, homely deities never worshipped at any great cost or with any display. And as to Apollo, though he was one of the Olympian crowd, yet it was in the conception of Apollo that the pagan world made its nearest approach to what the idea of deity means to us. All through Horace's writing Apollo stands for enlightenment, for poetry, for humane government instead of force, for the arts of peace instead of the brutality of war. It is no accident that Horace's highest representation of the work of Augustus is that he is the servant of Apollo; and to this form of exhortation Augustus gratefully gave heed.

In an Ode written in 17 B.C. Horace invites the chorus of noble youths and maidens to join in singing the hymn he had written for the Saecular Festival.

---

[1] It offers a striking contrast to the spoliation of the temple of Capitoline Jove which Horace denounced in *Odes*, 3.3.49. The thief was almost certainly the Triumvir Crassus in 55 B.C. (Plin. xxxiii, 14) — Augustus (Suet. *Aug.* 30) deposited a large sum there (as compensation to Jove?). For Horace's view of statues see 4.2.20 and 4.8.13, and 4.9.28; besides 3.30.1.

'Tis Phoebus, Phoebus fills my tongue
  With minstrel art and minstrel fires:
Come, noble youths and maidens sprung
  From noble sires,

.   .   .   .

Sing of Latona's glorious son,
  Sing of night's queen with crescent horn,
Who speeds the months in joy to run
  And swells the corn.
And happy brides shall say, "'Twas mine,
  When years the century's birthday brought,
To chant the festal hymn divine
  By Horace taught." [1]

Nupta iam dices: Ego dis amicum
Saeculo festas referente luces
Reddidi carmen docilis modorum
  Vatis Horati.

Horace's last word on public matters is to claim for himself the title of *Vates* 'seer.' And if by a seer we mean one whose teaching has helped to bring about the consummation he foretells, then assuredly few men have lived who could claim it with better right.

[1] The version is slightly modified from Conington's.

IV

POETRY AND GOVERNMENT

A Study of the Power of Vergil [1]

The last lecture of this course is to deal with what, I venture to hold, is far the greatest of the sources of the power which ancient Rome has exercised upon humanity. In point of chronology, I might have spoken of Vergil almost at any point of the series, for his life extended from 70 to 19 B.C. Yet in him more than in any other writer was summed up the best of what the ancient world has bequeathed to us; so that it is appropriate to study him last. We do not perhaps most commonly think of Vergil as having held any power in the sphere of politics, but are content to study him as a poet and a great interpreter of life. Yet he lived in a momentous epoch, and the influence which he exerted upon the course of its history is well worth study too. What contribution did Vergil make to the government of the Roman Empire and of the world?

The principles of government of which I am to speak are universally esteemed, in theory; the only question about them is how far in any time they have been or can yet be applied. At one epoch they were adopted by those in power more conspicuously than they have since been at any similar crisis; and I believe it can be shown that these principles, newer then than they are now, were first impressed upon the government of an empire, not by statesmen, but by poets. And if we admit that they are still important, we may be willing to study this for a little and to see how poetry once translated itself into action; how the fruit of reflection be-

[1] This lecture is based on my Presidential Address to the Classical Association of England and Wales in January, 1928, with some modifications to fit it for its place in the present course of lectures, and to embody the results of studies which have appeared since the address was first delivered. The stanza quoted at the end is from Sir William Watson's *Lacrimae Musarum*.

came the food of a new social order, and the thought of philosophers and historians came to mould the imagination of men who were governing the world.

In one sense we cannot discover much that is new. We know that the founder of the Roman Empire between his nineteenth and thirty-fourth years, that is, between 44 and 29 B.C., went through a process of enlightenment, which completely changed his conduct; and how far this change was due to the influence of Horace was the theme of my last lecture. Today let us consider the political thought to which Vergil, in his own ways, gave utterance, and see how it was embodied in the foundations of the Empire.

One difficulty meets us at the outset. We shall find more evidence than has yet been noticed, of what Vergil felt about public affairs, scattered through the whole of his writings, from his schoolboy poem, the *Culex*,[1] to the latest book of the *Aeneid*; and many of his comments were published long after the events to which they relate. Can we then, you may ask, gather from them what Vergil thought while the events were happening? If, for example, in the *Aeneid* he gravely censures things which Julius Caesar did, was this disapproval expressed soon enough to have any effect?

It is well to be warned of this objection; but two considerations will clear our path. First, that the period in which Vergil's influence was powerful began at least as early as 41 B.C., ten years before the battle of Actium, and extended over the whole reign of Augustus; hence the precise date at which any particular utterance of Vergil's became public does not matter much. We may be sure that what Vergil felt about any event was known to Maecenas, and through him, if not directly, to Octavian, long before it received final expression in poetic form. Secondly, and chiefly, although it is true that some of Vergil's political opinions received fuller expression as his thought ripened, yet there is no one of those with which we are now concerned which is not clearly represented in both the *Eclogues* and the *Georgics*. There is less than no indication that his political feeling was changed by

[1] See ll. 10, 60–65, 80–81; and with them l. 26.

the course of events (and in this he differs from Horace). On the contrary, it was the course of events that was profoundly changed by what Vergil felt.

Another difficulty is more serious because it lies not in the ancient evidence, but in our own minds. Of this I beg your leave to speak frankly. I am told that the late Charles Spurgeon used to say, criticising a habit of some of his more timid brethren which he called "preaching to the ventilator," i. e. of fixing their gaze on the ceiling instead of on their audience, that he often wished there was a sinner in the ventilator! Whether there is anyone within reach of my voice who is conscious of the weakness against which I am going to plead, I cannot tell; but that there are many people guilty of it in our schools I know by painful experience as an examiner. There is a certain curious cynicism which seems to haunt a scholar when he is called upon to form a judgement on public affairs, past or present — a cynicism which is really nothing but the dread of inexperienced persons to be detected in thinking too well of human nature; and this is reinforced by what seems a similar bias in historians who love to attribute everything good to men of action and everything feeble to men of thought. From all this there has grown up a quite gratuitous prejudice about the relations of Vergil, Horace, and Livy to Octavian. We are apt to think of him as Augustus, "the venerable," from the first; and to forget how many years he took in even beginning to deserve the name.

In the light of the evidence, some of which we shall examine, no reasonable mind can doubt that those great writers were the source and centre of what was good in the new Empire. But I am well aware that however plainly the evidence may be set forth, there will always remain a multitude of blinking eyes and shaking heads, of pedagogues counting themselves uncommonly wise when they are only uncommonly small, who say to themselves and to their unlucky pupils: "Of course, we know what these court-poets were; they only wrote what they were told to write, and they were paid for writing it." This is cant, and cheap cant, whether it comes from some professor in an ancient university or from humbler founts of darkness.[1] Scrutinise the evidence, test it, sift it every way you will; but do not run away from it because you are too lazy and too timid to believe in the power of ideas. *Cuius aures clausae sunt ad ueritatem, illi salus est desperanda.* There is no hope for those who shut their ears to the truth.

Our concern to-day is with Vergil; and so far as the limits of time allow my object is to make clear, on the one hand, how plainly he rebuked what he saw to be evil in the government of his day, and how hard he pleaded for deeper reflection; and on the other hand, how precisely, painfully, and literally Octavian learnt to embody Vergil's teaching in his own acts.

The evils which oppressed the world in Vergil's boyhood are familiar.[2] In the chaos of decaying governments and competing proconsuls, we find here and there a high-minded Rutilius or Cicero striving to moderate the forces of discord; but in the governing circle as a whole we look in vain for more than one idea — the idea of forcible personal power, won by any means, and exercised without scruple. In Caesar's *Gallic War* it is difficult to find any point of view but that of the soldier, the adventurer, the partisan politician.

One of the most violent of many attempts to "collar" the Empire — if I may use a schoolboy's phrase for a series of puerile designs — the conspiracy of Catiline, was suppressed when Vergil was a child. Familiar as we are with the story of that Etruscan murderer, I suspect that not all of us could say, offhand, where and how he is mentioned by Vergil. Yet his name appears in a famous passage which celebrates the triumph of Augustus and the protection which the gods had given to Rome. Among the scenes upon the shield of Aeneas, one is the picture of Catiline[3] in hell; this Vergil put in to represent the dangers from treachery which Rome had sur-

---

[1] Often some ignorance of Latin usage has given excuse for misunderstanding; such ignorance, for example, as has allowed us to take 'proud' as the nearest English equivalent of the Latin *superbus* instead of 'overbearing, cruel,' which the Latin word used of persons always implies; the last Tarquin was expelled for his cruelty, not for his pride.

[2] See p. 9 f. and p. 37 ff. *supra*.

[3] *Aeneid* viii. 667–669.

vived. It is the only human image wholly [1] black in all the design. What other poet would have included such a recollection? Yet to set a dark background behind a scene of thanksgiving was no new combination in Vergil's mind; for in his first celebration of Actium at the beginning of Book III of the *Georgics* one of the figures which is to stand on the face of the temple which the poet is to build is that of Hatred (*Inuidia*) cowering before the Furies and their chastisement. The defeat of Catiline was followed in only three years by the next conspiracy, that of Pompey, Crassus, and Caesar, whose ill deeds, as Seeley long ago pointed out, are condemned at the end of the Second Book of the *Georgics*.

Vergil's plainest reference to the Civil Wars is of course in Book VI of the *Aeneid* where Anchises addresses Julius and Pompey; and there is stern condemnation in the line of Ennius which Vergil adopts, *Neu patriae ualidas in uiscera uertite uires*. But some fifteen years earlier at the end [2] of Book I of the *Georgics* how are the great victories of Pharsalia and Philippi described? Both were triumphs for Caesar's party; but by Vergil both are counted as national calamities. They are crimes that have 'turned the world upside down' (*euerso saeclo*); they have embodied the curse of heaven upon a shameless age.

Observe, too, the respect which Vergil shows for the vanquished party in his references to Cato of Utica, the only character in history known by the name of the place at which he took his own life. On the shield of Aeneas Cato occupies a place contrasted with that given to Catiline.[3] The only Roman whom Vergil thought worthy to be a judge in the next world was the man who killed himself after the battle of Thapsus rather than live to see Caesar's triumph.[4] It was

---

[1] Here as by Horace (*Odes*, i. 37) the tragic but queenly figure of Cleopatra is described with abhorrence, it is true, but not without a certain touch of respectful pity, shown especially in the beautiful image of Nile welcoming back the defeated fleet to refuge in his blue waters. It can hardly be doubted that the episode of the Shield belongs as a whole to the earlier of the stages of composition that can be recognised in the *Aeneid* — certainly before Book VI — and it is possible that the Cleopatra passage was at least drafted before her death.

[2] i. 489–500.   [3] *Aeneid*, viii. 670.

[4] There is another reference to Cato in a passage where he is not named but where the commentators on Plutarch have identified him through the likeness of the story

certainly Vergil who led Dante to promote Cato, somewhat late in his career, to a post of honour at the Gate of Purgatory. That is a distinction to which Augustus never attained; but he did in the end learn to forgive and promote a number of his old enemies.[1]

After Thapsus came the chapter of romance, or rather the second and final chapter of it, in Julius Caesar's career, which underlies the greatest tragedy of the *Aeneid*, namely, Caesar's capture by Cleopatra and her life with him in Rome.[2] Nothing in the conduct of their rulers in all that troubled age had more deeply impressed the imagination of the Roman people than the degradation which they felt in this alliance. What did Vergil feel? He calls[3] it *nefas*, 'the horror of an Egyptian wife.' And it is not too much to say that having once conceived the story of Dido's love for Aeneas, Vergil had no power to make it end in anything but tragedy. First Julius Caesar and then Antony had fallen because they had deserted their Roman consorts for love of Cleopatra. Aeneas must be rescued, however sternly, from that fate. That is one part of what Dido's story meant.

In Eclogue IX, some years afterwards, the poet could celebrate sincerely the memory of the great conqueror, who was also the benefactor of North Italy; and his conviction that so potent a spirit must be somewhere still living[4] and still potent, was a noteworthy contribution to public feeling. But it offered small comfort for the future of Rome; nor had Vergil yet any comfort to offer. For good or ill the Dictator was gone; but worse dangers were present to every mind in the light of the massacres of 43 and 41, and the confiscations

---

to Vergil's picture of the statesman revered for his goodness and public service who quieted a multitude as Neptune calmed the sea. It is conceivable that Vergil was present in this scene in the Forum during Cato's praetorship of 54 B.C.; in any case he must have known it by report. See Plut. *Cato Minor*, xliv; Verg., *Aeneid*, i. 151.

[1] Some of these are addressed, as we have seen (p. 54 *supra*), in Book II of Horace's *Odes*, especially the Pompeius of Ode VII, where the lines

quis te redonauit Quiritem
dis patriis Italoque caelo?

are a restrained and yet graceful reference to Augustus, worthy of Vergil himself.

[2] See p. 14 *supra*.   [3] *Aeneid* viii. 688.

[4] *Ecce Dionaei processit Caesaris astrum*, ll. 47 ff. But I no longer venture to identify Daphnis with Caesar; see Leon Herrmann's *Masques et Visages dans les Bucoliques*, Brussels, 1930, and my remarks upon it in *Class. Rev.*, 1931, p. 29.

that followed and continued for two years more until every farmer in Italy (so the historians plainly tell [1] us) had been either expelled from his farm or had paid a heavy ransom.

In his First Eclogue Vergil condemns this cruelty in strong terms. The cause that afflicts the fellow-citizens of Tityrus, and that drove all Cremona and part of Mantua into exile, is openly called the Civil War, and the offenders are 'barbarian soldiers.' This censure is clear, and Octavian could only be exempted from it on the ground that he was forced to consent to Antony's wishes. His own promise proved ineffective even to save Vergil, who, as we learn from the Ninth Eclogue and otherwise, was finally turned out with some risk to his life.

Nevertheless the horizon is somehow brighter in the Ninth Eclogue and we feel that something has happened. The Civil War is no longer mentioned; and although Menalcas, that is, Vergil, has lost his farm, he looks forward to singing 'better songs.' In the light of the Fourth Eclogue we see what it was that changed the prospect. It was the first work of Maecenas in Roman politics, the peace of Brundisium in 40 B.C., one effect of which was to separate Octavian's power from Antony's. It kindled in Vergil's mind the wonderful hopes of a new era which he linked with the expected birth [2] of an heir to Octavian, the child that proved to be Julia.[3]

The fruits of the Fourth Eclogue in the religious history of the world lie outside our theme today. But it is certain that no Roman could read such a prophecy without being moved by its confident hope; and by the feeling that in some mystic way that young ruler (still only 23) had been lifted above the level of everyday; that from now onwards he had received an inspired commission to be the saviour of Rome.

How was he to fulfil it? One answer appears in the prelude to the *Georgics*, where Vergil, after surveying different

[1] Dio Cassius, xlviii. 6; Appian, *B.C.* v. 22.

[2] See *The Messianic Eclogue of Vergil*, Mayor, Fowler, and Conway (1906).

[3] This I still believe to be far the likeliest answer to the riddle, despite Prof. L. Herrmann's ingenious pleas for Marcellus. One of these, the inference from *facta parentis legere* (l. 29) that the child's father was no longer living, seemed to me fairly strong until I remembered that it is a sign of the boy's growth. He would hear of his father's achievements long before he could read about them.

themes [1] which he might choose, concludes that the best he can do is to 'take pity on the men of the country' and show them 'the way which they do not know.'

Has it ever struck you what a strange description this is of the farmers of Italy? Why should the Emperor and the poet be needed to help the farmers to know their own business? The riddle is easily answered. Most of them are the very people who have turned out Vergil and thousands more from their homes; they are the old soldiers of the Triumvirs, pensioned with grants of land, but knowing little how to till it, and many of them caring less. The rest are the old farmers, crushed by heavy blackmail, or transferred by force to inferior land. Such were the conditions which were leaving the fields to go to ruin.

That is why the *Georgics* are even more an appeal to sentiment than a treatise of instruction. The new farmers, and such few of the old farmers as were left, needed to take fresh heart if the glory of the countryside was to come back. Those who would treat as irrelevant every passage in the *Georgics* which awakens enthusiasm for a farmer's life, show a double ignorance, of Vergil and of his times.

But what of the Emperor? Was his share in the work confined to accepting this poetical tribute of hope? Augustus answered this question himself, first in act, and then in word in his own public autobiography, the *Monumentum Ancyranum*. [2] There he tells us that he settled three hundred thousand veterans on the land: and that alone of Roman conquerors he had paid for all the land he gave, the cost being 860,000,000 sesterces (£7,400,000 sterling or $37,000,000 at the lowest computation). The man who did this after Actium was a different being from the Triumvir who consented to the destruction of Cremona, and the master of the shambles [3] at Perusia.

We have reached the period of Actium, the years before which were full of dread. Two fears stood out above the rest,

---

[1] Under the guise of different realms over which Octavian might be expected to extend his patronage; see *Proceedings of the Classical Association*, Manchester, 1906, p. 35; *Harvard Lectures on the Vergilian Age*, p. 70 f.

[2] See p. 51 *supra*.   [3] See p. 51 *supra*.

the first, lest Antony should become sole master of the Empire, the second, lest the seat of the Empire should be taken away from Rome. This latter point has been fully discussed, and I will only add here that it needed courage to oppose a project which at some time must have been entertained by Augustus; no lesser person could need the united efforts of Vergil, Horace, and Livy [1] to dissuade him.

On the other point, about Antony, some scholars have been strangely in doubt as to what Vergil felt. Besides other references of a more general type, there is one passage whose full significance has not yet, I believe, been realised, in the description of the giant robber Cacus, whose punishment and death at the hands of Hercules was the delight of our schooldays. Recent study has shown that behind the grim picture lies a grave meaning. No reader of Norden's splendid commentary on Book VI of the *Aeneid* can doubt that everywhere in that book, and in the later books, the work of Hercules, no less than that of Aeneas, is meant to be understood as setting the type for the work of Augustus. It follows that the enemies whom Hercules and Aeneas subdued are also typical; like the giants in Horace, they are the anarchic forces which Octavian had to conquer. Now one detail in the picture of Cacus must have served to identify him to every Roman reader. In the description of any bandit's cave we expect, no doubt, to find traces of rapine, stolen goods, lifted cattle, perhaps the body of some shepherd newly slain; but why need the bandit mutilate as well as murder? Why did Cacus cut off the heads of his victims and fasten them up over the entrance to his cave? Surely they did not add to the amenities of his country residence? But did it add, let us ask in grave earnest, to the amenities of the Roman Forum to see Cicero's head impaled on the rostra? Could any Roman who had seen that head there in that black December of 43 B.C., read Vergil's story, without knowing that Antony had been another Cacus, that Antony had breathed out fire and slaughter, that Antony had at last reaped his reward? Antony, like Turnus and Cacus, could not submit to the order

[1] See *New Studies of a Great Inheritance*, 2nd Ed., London, 1931, p. 60.

of civilised life. It became the boast of Octavian to live as a citizen, a first citizen, no doubt, but a citizen always; and Antony would not.

But perhaps you will remind me that in that age Antony was not the only person who pleased himself by contemplating the head of an enemy. Not to speak of Herod and Salome, what had Octavian himself done with the head of Brutus who had killed himself at Philippi? Octavian had had it cut off and sent to Rome to be laid at the foot of the Dictator's statue.[1] In the year before that, i. e. in 43, he had signed the proclamation of the Proscription [2] offering 2,500 drachmae (£100) apiece for the head of every one of 2,000 Roman citizens. That was not in the heat of battle, but in cold blood, round a table; and if Octavian had a share in the guilt, as undoubtedly he had, then he has also some share in Vergil's censure, though he did not exhibit the trophies of murder, as Antony did. It is the way of a great poet to make men hate ill deeds, not by denouncing the criminal but by depicting his crime.

Just the same is true in another case of which I must only speak in passing — the tragedy of Dido. That lay in the fact [3] that Juno and Venus made her the tool of their political schemes. They were inspired by national jealousy, by the narrow hostility which supposes that the prosperity of a neighbouring nation is a danger and an offence, a belief which Europe had certainly not outgrown in 1914. What is the outcome of it in Vergil's story? The ruin and death of a great queen? Is that the answer? Yes, but that is not the end; the end is that invoked by her curse, strangely unnoticed or foolishly glossed over by the commentators — the curse that took shape, to Vergil's mind, in the Punic Wars — one the most dangerous and the other the most cruel in which Rome was ever engaged. 'That,' says Vergil, 'is the fruit of your racial jealousies; and that too is what comes of using human affection for a pawn in your political game.'

---

[1] Suet. *Aug.* 13, where examples of his inhuman cruelty (at this period) will be found (cf. p. 51 *supra*).

[2] Appian, *B.C.* iv. 8 (p. 50 *supra*).

[3] See *New Studies of a Great Inheritance*, c. vi: "The Place of Dido in History," where the whole question is discussed.

Even Augustus lived long enough to become what we should call today a good European, not merely a good Roman; and he lived long enough also to see the fruit of some of the evil he had sown in treating his sister Octavia, his daughter Julia, his faithful admiral Agrippa, and the patient Tiberius, to mention no others, as so many ciphers in his dynastic calculations. Almost the last public act of Augustus which we have recorded seems to have been a pathetic effort [1] at reparation for one of his earlier cruelties. At the age of seventy-six he sailed to the island of Planasia (half-way to Corsica) to see his banished grandson Agrippa; and had Augustus lived another year, it seems likely that that unhappy prince would have been restored, instead of being left to the tender mercies of the new Emperor.

Besides the passages we have already noticed there is one other mark of sorrow over the course of public affairs which Vergil was constrained to express, in his own way. The form which Vergil's mourning took was so characteristically silent that there have been even those who doubted if it was a sign of mourning at all. Yet no one who approaches the Fourth Book of the *Georgics* with an open mind, after reading the others, can possibly doubt that there must be some grave reason for the startling break in the middle of that Book. Why does Vergil suddenly depart from his theme — the cultivation of bees — and entangle us in a chain of three mythical stories, linking them to one another, and to the bees, by mere gossamer threads, and making only a half-hearted attempt to connect the end with the beginning?

There is not the least reason to doubt what Servius tells us, that this Book originally ended with the praises of Egypt and of Gallus, Vergil's bosom-friend and his partner in his early poetry, who was then governor of Egypt, and who, having unhappily displeased Augustus by a display [2] of boyish van-

---

[1] Quite possibly suggested to him by the historian Livy, if I am right in thinking that the dramatic scene in which Philip V, Perseus, and Demetrius are the actors in Book XL had reference to intrigues at the court of Augustus. See "A Graeco-Roman Tragedy" (*John Rylands' Library Bulletin*, July, 1926). If so, the whole story was a remarkable foreshadowing of the murder of young Agrippa by Tiberius.

[2] The record of this in his own trilingual inscription was discovered at Philae about thirty years ago; see *New Studies of a Great Inheritance*, c. v.

ity, committed suicide. One can hardly doubt that the displeasure of Augustus had been invoked by courtiers jealous of the young poet's high promotion, eager to put the worst colour on the imprudent things he did. Suetonius tells us that Augustus was deeply grieved when he heard of Gallus's death, and bemoaned his own lot in being the only man in the world who could never afford to be angry with a friend. In the regret of Augustus some part was surely due to his consciousness of what the death of Gallus would mean to Vergil. Vergil's silent destruction of what was probably the most perfect piece of handiwork which he ever framed, was indeed a tribute to his grief; but it carried also a grave reflection on the conditions of empire which had led to the tragedy. Nor can we doubt that among the influences which softened the temper of the Emperor and inclined him to more merciful judgement as he grew older, one at least must have been the sorrow which his treatment of Gallus had inflicted on the poet he revered.

This was the tragic turning-point, the βαλβὶς λυπηρά of Vergil's life. No more after this the glowing hopes or the merry banter of the *Eclogues*, no more the happy pictures of country life in the *Georgics*. The *Aeneid* begins with the question of questions,[1]

tantaene animis caelestibus irae?

and ends with a sigh [2] of pity for the fate of the last enemy of peace.

So far the political comments we have traced are of a negative kind, though such as it required courage to pronounce. Let us ask now what positive contribution Vergil made to political thought.

To answer the question, "What were Vergil's ideas of government?" is, of course, not difficult: piety, amnesty, conciliation, humanity, simplicity, sympathy, self-sacrifice, natural affection — all these things every reader of any Book of Vergil's must know. I must be content to draw attention

---

[1] I owe this point to a lecture of my colleague Prof. W. B. Anderson.
[2] See *The Messianic Eclogue of Vergil*, c. i *ad fin.*

to one or two passages charged with a special significance at the time they were written.

That Vergil hated war we know; but how practical his interest was we sometimes forget. How many of us have taken seriously the fact that Vergil went to Brundisium with Maecenas in 37 B.C. to help make peace with Antony and Sextus Pompey? In the *Aeneid*, the climax to which the story of Aeneas is brought is the reconciliation of the enemy Juno on fair and friendly terms, by which the extremes of national feeling on both sides are sacrificed; the Latins are to keep their name and language, but accept a Trojan king. The most beautiful of the monuments which Octavian set up in Rome was the Ara Pacis, whose name, not by accident, recalls the crowning point of the ideal which Vergil set up for the Roman people,

> pacisque imponere morem,
> parcere subiectis et debellare superbos,

'to implant the fashion of peace, showing mercy to those who submit and subduing the cruel.'

Horace and Livy repeat [1] almost verbally the same golden rule; and Augustus puts it in the forefront of his autobiography. And it was not in the *Aeneid* that Vergil first proclaimed this creed. It is implied in the *Eclogues* and in every Book of the *Georgics*; and becomes explicit in a startling phrase in the description given of Octavian's work in the epilogue to that poem.

For what is it that Octavian is there said to be doing for which the world is to thank him? Not that he has slain his thousands and ten thousands, not that he has led a multitude of kings into captivity: it is that the peoples among whom he is moving welcome his rule; that he is giving laws to willing nations, and in that way is earning immortal honour, *uictorque uolentes per populos dat iura uiamque adfectat Olympo*, lines to which our own Francis Bacon [2] pointed as the "best

---

[1] Hor. *Carm. Saec.* 51: bellante prior, iacentem lenis in hostem.

Livy, xxx. 42. 17: populum Romanum plus paene parcendo uictis quam uincendo imperium auxisse. For Augustus' words see p. 52 *supra*.

[2] *Adv. of Learning*, i. 8, 3.

of human honours." In this teaching Vergil brings us, as in
fact he brought Octavian, a long way from the Gallic Wars,
and still further from the massacres of 43 and 41; yet it was
written in 30 B.C. before Octavian returned to Rome, while
no one yet knew what he would do.

The humanity of Vergil needs no demonstration. But we
do not realise how direct an effect it had upon the Emperor's
government. Take one simple and concrete example. In the
gladiatorial combats Augustus laid down the rule [1] that the
right to appeal for mercy should never be denied to a defeated combatant. And out of sixty-two shows which he records [2] that he gave to the people, only eight were of gladiators. Remembering this, we see a new and real importance
in the conspicuous humanity of the games which Aeneas
held, as contrasted with the parallel pictures in Homer [3] and
even in Theocritus. [4]

The simplicity of life which Octavian practised — especially the comparatively humble house [5] in which he chose
to live, reflects the picture of the aged Greek king Evander
whom Vergil represents as his predecessor on the Palatine.
When Evander welcomes Aeneas to his humble roof, his first
word bids his guest 'dare to despise wealth' and so make
himself worthy of a divine visit, such as Hercules had paid to
Evander.

And there is one example of Vergil's understanding of the
simple life of the poor and his sympathy with it, of which
Dr. Arthur Verrall first pointed out the meaning.

In the Eighth Book of the *Aeneid* Vergil relates how Vul-
can set about to make divine armour for Aeneas; but what is
the comparison which he chooses to describe the hour of the
night at which the god rises to begin the work? Of this
Dr. Verrall wrote in 1908: "Neither Homer, nor any known
author before Vergil, nor perhaps any since, would have put
the simile here, or could have touched it to so tender an
issue."

---

[1] Suet. *Aug.* 45, gladiatores sine missione edi prohibuit.
[2] *Mon. Anc.*, 22–24.   [3] *Iliad*, xxiii. 802 ff.
[4] Theocr. *Idyll*, xxii, e. g. 130, 200 ff., contrasted with *Aen.* v. 461 ff.
[5] Suet. *Aug.* 72.

Let me quote Dr. Verrall's rendering: [1] 'At the hour when a woman awakens the slumbering ashes of her fire, a woman on whom lies the burden to live by her distaff and spinning of thread; of night-time she makes work-time; and plies her maids with the long, long task till dawn, that she may be able to keep her honour for her husband and to rear her little children.'

> cum femina primum,
> Cui tolerare colo uitam tenuique Minerua
> Impositum, cinerem et sopitos suscitat ignes,
> Noctem addens operi; famulasque ad lumina longo
> Exercet penso, castum ut seruare cubile
> Coniugis et possit paruos educere natos.

Why this sudden transition from the dignity and glamour of the epic story to the picture of the cottage of an Italian peasant, whose wife has a hard task to feed and clothe her children and to keep her home unspotted? Why, but to suggest unmistakably that the greatest powers of the universe are no greater than the impulse of human affection? And that the power of this may be seen in the humblest dwelling and in menial work? That all the beauty of the shield of Aeneas, all its promise of the greatness of Rome, of the conquests by which good government was to be brought to an afflicted world, was to be measured — how? In terms of a mother's care for her husband and her children. Vergil's peasant-mother, in her day and degree, has her place in that divine circle of which the centre is in the home of the Carpenter of Nazareth.

Last of all, let me ask you to consider the rare occasions on which in the *Aeneid* Vergil speaks in the first person directly to his reader? There are only six such passages; one of them we have already noticed at the outset of the *Aeneid* where he marvels at the irrational anger by which the gods appear to be moved. Four others are brief prefaces of the Homeric type where Vergil begs for special inspiration at special points of the story, such as the descent into the Underworld. There is one and only one in which the poet himself avows any confi-

---

[1] National Home-Reading Union: *Supplementary Course*, 68 (1908), *Vergil*, p. 25.

dence of his own in the permanence of what he has written; and that is the unique outburst of feeling after the death of Nisus and Euryalus in the Ninth Book.

We all know how the two boys had volunteered to make their way by night through the enemies' lines, in order to fetch Aeneas; how, after some success at first, Euryalus is captured, and Nisus, in a desperate attempt to rescue him, perishes too. The story ends with the scene in which the heads of the two lads, impaled on spears, are carried by the enemy under the walls of the Trojan camp before the eyes of the mother of Euryalus, who is led away into mourning by honoured commanders of the Trojan host. If we had been asked to guess with what words the poet would begin an apostrophe of his own to young men so cut off, which of us would not have expected phrases of reverent pity and of sorrow? But Vergil's word is of congratulation, of triumph: *fortunati*, 'blessed are ye.' It is the third beatitude of Vergil. The first is in the great passage in Book II of the *Georgics*: 'Blessed are the husbandmen if they have learnt to know their wealth'; and the second a little further on: 'Blessed is the poet who knows the gods of the countryside'; and here we have the third, 'Blessed are ye, Nisus and Euryalus,' that is, 'Blessed are the young who give their lives for their fellows.'

> 'O happy both! If aught my song avails,
> No day shall blot you from remembering years
> While by the Capitol's unmoving rock
> Aeneas' house shall stand, and he whom Rome
> Calls Father, gives commandment to the world.'

> Fortunati ambo! Si quid mea carmina possunt
> nulla dies unquam memori uos eximet aeuo;
> dum domus Aeneae Capitoli immobile saxum
> accolet, imperiumque pater Romanus habebit.

The pledge has been more than fulfilled. Neither Capitol nor Vatican now commands the world. But this promise, which Vergil made to no one else, marks the temper of those two boys as the real foundation of the Kingdom of Peace that he longed for, the spiritual Rome.

Such was the teaching of one poet at a great crisis, such the power he wielded to revive a faith in goodness in the hearts of his countrymen and their ruler; and if we even dimly realise what that power was, what that power is, can we think it superfluous to study that poet's work, to cherish Vergil as a living teacher today? Must not those who have any care for the things that were dear to him, for peace, for justice, for conciliation, for government by consent, for arbitration in place of war, for the mutual understanding of nations, realise that in the great Classical writers we have a standard of appeal, which though it may not transcend or equal other influences that have moved mankind, is far less subject to question than any other? True it is that common efforts to discover the secrets of natural knowledge, creating almost by the way new means of intercourse and new powers of combating disease, do bring together workers from different nations; long may such happy co-operation continue and increase! But it is, alas, also true that the competition for discoveries which may have enormous financial value, or enormous capacity for mischief in war, may sharpen rather than soften the jealousies of nations, may foment rather than allay the causes of strife.

And the same dangers of division beset us, in a more insidious shape, when we appeal to men's highest motives. A student who was once asked to what church he subscribed, replied proudly, "I belong to the church of Christ, founded in Texas in 1868." Such an answer, and others like it, can, of course, only be made by a man who knows no Greek. In our own tongue, even the sublime conceptions of religion may wear a provincial dress or a partisan badge; and the same is true in every living language. But the great ideals of the old world, indissolubly linked with the primitive record of Christianity, are preserved for us in letters of gold, in language that escapes all change; they stand behind and beyond our local habits, and our local forms of creed. To them the peoples of the civilised world look back with reverence; and by them the nations of the future may still be inspired and brought nearer to each other. Let us not think lightly, then, of the old high road which the course of European education still leaves open before every new age. Let us see to it that our successors may have the privilege that has been given to us of hearing the great voices of that older time speak in their own accents across the silent years, of being quickened by them to know the gold from the dross, of learning from them what is simple, what is high, what is human, what is true.

> Captains and conquerors leave a little dust,
> And kings a dubious legend of their reign;
> The swords of Caesar, they are less than rust:
> The poet doth remain.

INDEX

INDEX